MW00565693

# Westward Expansion and Migration

## American History Series

**Authors:**      Cindy Barden and Maria Backus

**Consultants:**   Schyrlet Cameron and Suzanne Myers

**Editors:**       Mary Dieterich and Sarah M. Anderson

**Proofreader:**   Margaret Brown

COPYRIGHT © 2011 Mark Twain Media, Inc.

ISBN 978-1-58037-584-9

Printing No. CD-404138

Mark Twain Media, Inc., Publishers
Distributed by Carson-Dellosa Publishing LLC

Visit us at www.carsondellosa.com

# Table of Contents

# Table of Contents (cont.)

# About the American History Series

*Westward Expansion and Migration* is one of the books in Mark Twain Media's new *American History Series.* This book focuses on the exploration of Lewis and Clark, the expansion of the United States across the continent, and the California Gold Rush. Students will see how settlers packed up their families, made the long journey across the country, and settled in new territories. This series is designed to provide students in grades 5 through 8 with opportunities to explore the significant events and people that make up American history. Other books in the series include *Exploration, Revolution, and Constitution*; *Slavery, Civil War, and Reconstruction*; and *Industrialization to the Great Depression*.

The books in this series are written for classroom teachers, parents, and students. They are designed as stand-alone material for classrooms and home schooling. Also, the books can be used as supplemental material to enhance the history curriculum in the classroom, independent study, or as a tutorial at home.

The text in each book is presented in an easy-to-read format that does not overwhelm the struggling reader. Vocabulary words are boldfaced. Each book provides challenging activities that enable students to explore history, geography, and social studies topics. The activities promote reading, critical thinking, and writing skills. As students learn about the people who influenced history, they will draw conclusions; write opinions; compare and contrast historical events, people, and places; analyze cause and effect; and improve mapping skills. The research and technology activities will further increase their knowledge and understanding of historical events by using reference sources of the Internet.

The easy-to-follow format of the books facilitate planning for the diverse learning styles and skill levels of middle-school students. National standards addressed in each unit are identified and listed at the beginning of the book, simplifying lesson preparation. Each unit provides the teacher with alternative methods of instruction: reading exercises for concept development, simple hands-on activities to strengthen understanding of concepts, and challenging research activities to provide opportunities for students to expand learning. A bibliography of suggested resources is included to assist the teacher in finding additional resources or to provide a list of recommended reading for students who want to expand their knowledge.

The *American History Series* supports the No Child Left Behind (NCLB) Act. The books promote student knowledge and understanding of history concepts. The content and activities are designed to strengthen the understanding of historical events that have shaped our nation. The units are correlated with the National History Standards for United States History (NHS) and Curriculum Standards for Social Studies (NCSS).

# Unit Planning Guide

## National Standards Matrix

Each unit of study in the book *Westward Expansion and Migration* is designed to strengthen American history literacy skills and is correlated with the National History Standards (NHS) and Curriculum Standards for Social Studies (NCSS).

| | Unit 1 | Unit 2 | Unit 3 |
|---|:---:|:---:|:---:|
| **National History Standards** | | | |
| Standard 1: Chronological Thinking | X | X | X |
| Standard 2: Historical Comprehension | X | X | X |
| Standard 3: Historical Analysis and Interpretation | X | X | X |
| Standard 4. Historical Research Capabilities | X | X | X |
| **Curriculum Standards for Social Studies** | | | |
| Standard 1: Culture | X | X | X |
| Standard 2: Time, Continuity, and Change | X | X | X |
| Standard 3: People, Places, and Environments | X | X | X |
| Standard 4: Individual Development and Identity | X | X | X |
| Standard 5: Individuals, Groups, and Institutions | X | X | |
| Standard 6: Power, Authority, and Governance | X | X | X |
| Standard 7: Production, Distribution, and Consumption | X | X | X |
| Standard 8: Science, Technology, and Society | X | X | X |
| Standard 9: Global Connections | X | | X |
| Standard 10: Civil Ideals and Practices | X | X | X |

# Suggested Resources

Dean, Arlan. *The Oregon Trail: From Independence, Missouri, to Oregon City, Oregon.* The Rosen Publishing Group, Inc.: New York. 2003.

Dean, Arlan. *The Santa Fe Trail: From Independence, Missouri, to Santa Fe, New Mexico.* The Rosen Publishing Group, Inc.: New York. 2003.

Friedman, Mel. *The Oregon Trail.* Childrens Press: New York. 2010.

Halpern, Monica. *Railroad Fever: Building the Transcontinental Railroad, 1830–1870.* National Geographic Children's Books: Des Moines, IA. 2004.

Huey, Lois Miner. *American Archaeology Uncovers the Westward Movement.* Marshall Cavendish Corporation: Tarrytown, NY. 2010.

Hunsaker, Joyce Badgley. *Seeing the Elephant: The Many Voices of the Oregon Trail.* Texas Tech University Press: Lubbock, TX. 2003.

Isserman, Maurice. *Exploring North America, 1800–1900.* Chelsea House Publishers: New York. 2009.

Kalman, Bobbie, et. al. *Life in the Old West* series. Crabtree Publishing Company: New York. 1999.

Klobuchar, Lisa. *The History and Activities of the Wagon Trail.* Heinemann Library: Chicago. 2006.

Marsico, Katie. *The Trail of Tears: The Tragedy of the American Indians.* Benchmark Books: New York. 2009.

McNeese, Tim. *The Transcontinental Railroad and Westward Expansion: Chasing the American Frontier.* Enslow Publishers, Inc.: Berkeley Heights, NJ. 2006.

Moriarty, J.T. *Manifest Destiny.* The Rosen Publishing Group, Inc.: New York. 2005.

Olson, Tod. *How to Get Rich in the California Gold Rush.* National Geographic Society: Washington, D.C. 2008.

Olson, Tod. *How to Get Rich on the Oregon Trail.* National Geographic Society: Washington, D.C. 2009.

Orr, Tamra. *The Lewis and Clark Expedition.* The Rosen Publishing Group, Inc.: New York. 2004.

Payment, Simone. *The Pony Express.* The Rosen Publishing Group, Inc.: New York. 2005.

Porterfield, Jason. *The Homestead Act of 1862.* The Rosen Publishing Group, Inc.: New York. 2005.

Rivera, Sheila. *The California Gold Rush.* ABDO Publishing Company: Edina, MN. 2004.

Salas, Laura Purdie. *The Trail of Tears, 1838.* Capstone Press: Mankato, MN. 2003.

Schlaepfer, Gloria G. *The Louisiana Purchase.* Franklin Watts: London. 2005

Sioux, Tracee. *Immigrants and the Westward Expansion.* The Rosen Publishing Group, Inc.: New York. 2004.

Steele, Christy. *Cattle Ranching in the American West.* World Almanac Library: Milwaukee, WI. 2005.

Steele, Christy. *Famous Wagon Trails.* World Almanac Library: Milwaukee, WI. 2005.

Suen, Anastasia. *Trappers & Mountain Men.* Rourke Publishing Group: Vero Beach, FL. 2006.

# Time Line of the Lewis and Clark Expedition

**1770** William Clark is born in Virginia.

**1774** Meriwether Lewis is born in Virginia.

**1801** Lewis becomes President Jefferson's personal secretary.

**1803** The United States purchases the Louisiana Territory.

**1804** May 14          The expedition leaves St. Louis.

August 20      Sergeant Floyd dies of appendicitis near Sioux City, Iowa.

October 25     The expedition reaches the Mandan villages. They build Fort Mandan and stay for the winter.

**1805** April 7          They leave Fort Mandan and travel west on the Missouri River.

June 13         Lewis arrives at Great Falls on the Missouri River.

June 22         They begin the portage around Great Falls.

July 4            They complete the portage around Great Falls.

July 25          The expedition arrives at Three Forks on the Missouri River.

September     The expedition crosses the Rocky Mountains.

November     They build Fort Clatsop near the Pacific Ocean and stay for the winter.

**1806** March 23        The expedition leaves Fort Clatsop and heads home.

September 21    They arrive back in St. Louis.

**1807** Lewis becomes the Governor of the Louisiana Territory.

Clark becomes the Superintendent of Indian Affairs for the Louisiana Territory.

**UNIT ONE: LEWIS & CLARK**

Name: _____　Date: _____

# Lewis and Clark Time Line Activity

**Directions:** Number the events in order from 1 (first) to 10 (last). Use the time line for reference.

_____　A.　Lewis becomes the Governor of the Louisiana Territory.

_____　B.　The expedition crosses the Rocky Mountains.

_____　C.　The expedition leaves St. Louis.

_____　D.　The United States purchases the Louisiana Territory.

_____　E.　The expedition arrives at Three Forks on the Missouri River.

_____　F.　The expedition leaves Fort Clatsop and heads home.

_____　G.　They build Fort Clatsop near the Pacific Ocean and stay for the winter.

_____　H.　Sergeant Floyd dies of appendicitis near Sioux City, Iowa.

_____　I.　Lewis becomes President Jefferson's personal secretary.

_____　J.　Lewis arrives at Great Falls on the Missouri River.

**True or False:** Circle "T" for True or "F" for False.

1.　T　　F　　Clark becomes the Superintendent of Indian Affairs for the Louisiana Territory in 1807.

2.　T　　F　　The expedition of Lewis and Clark left St. Joseph in 1894.

3.　T　　F　　In 1805, the expedition builds Fort Clatsop near the Pacific Ocean and stays for the winter.

4.　T　　F　　Both Meriwether Lewis and William Clark were born in Virginia in 1774.

5.　T　　F　　The United States purchased the Louisiana Territory in 1805.

Name: _____ Date: _____

# Meriwether Lewis

Meriwether Lewis was born on a plantation near Charlottesville, Virginia, on August 18, 1774. When the American War of Independence began in 1775, his father, John Lewis, left home to fight against the British. His father died of pneumonia in 1779 while on leave from the war. His mother remarried a short time later, and the family moved to Georgia after the war.

There were no schools in Georgia in 1779, so Lewis had time to hunt, fish, and roam the woods. He became an excellent woodsman. Because he was interested in the plants in the area, his mother taught him how to make herbal medicines.

Lewis returned to Virginia when he was 13 to attend school. He also learned to manage the family's plantation that had been left to him.

By 1794, Lewis was ready for a change. When President George Washington asked for volunteers to help put down the Whiskey Rebellion, Lewis joined the Virginia militia. He enjoyed his experience in the militia, so he decided to join the regular army. He was then assigned to the rifle company in Fort Greenville, Ohio. It was there that he met and became a friend of Captain William Clark.

---

**Cause and Effect**

**Directions:** A **cause** is an event that produces a result. An **effect** is the result produced. Fill in the cause-and-effect chart below.

1. **Cause:** The American War of Independence began in 1775.

   **Effect:** _____

2. **Cause:** _____

   **Effect:** Lewis had time to hunt, fish, and roam the woods.

3. **Cause:** Lewis returned to Virginia.

   **Effect:** _____

4. **Cause:** _____

   **Effect:** Lewis joined the regular army.

---

Name: _____ Date: _____

# William Clark

William Clark was born near Richmond, Virginia, on August 1, 1770. All five of his older brothers fought against the British in the American War of Independence. When Clark was fourteen, his family moved to the western frontier. This is now present-day Kentucky. There were no schools there, so his older brothers helped him learn natural history and science.

At that time, forests covered Kentucky. Because Clark spent much of his time roaming the woods, he became highly skilled in hunting, fishing, tracking, camping, and land navigation.

Kentucky was also home to the Shawnee and Wabash tribes. Clark joined his older brother George to fight the natives who were upset that the white settlers were taking their land from them.

In 1789, Clark became a soldier and was eventually promoted to the rank of captain. While in the army, Clark learned to understand and respect the Native Americans. It was while he was commanding a rifle company in Ohio that Captain Clark met and became friends with Meriwether Lewis.

---

**Directions:** Fill in the chart below.

1. **Birth**

   Date: _____

   Place: _____

2. **Family Move**

   From: _____

   To: _____

3. **Education**

   Studied: _____

   _____

   _____

   _____

   _____

4. **Outdoor Skills**

   _____

   _____

   _____

   _____

5. **Military Service**

   Rank: _____

   _____

6. **Relationship With Native Americans**

   _____

   _____

   _____

---

Name: _____ Date: _____

# Lewis and Clark

**William Clark and Meriwether Lewis**

Meriwether Lewis was born in Virginia. He had five years of formal schooling. He also learned to hunt, fish, and make herbal medicines. He was an excellent amateur naturalist.

Before the expedition started, he studied medicine, botany, zoology, and celestial navigation. He was over six feet tall, had a slender build, and had dark hair. He was often moody and impatient. He preferred to be by himself rather than with other people. He had been a captain in the army.

William Clark was born in Virginia. Although he did not have much formal schooling, his older brothers helped him with his studies. He became an experienced geographer, map maker, nature artist, and riverboat man. He had excellent hunting, fishing, trapping, and camping skills. He was over six feet tall, had a stocky build, and had bright red hair. He was sociable and even-tempered. He had been a captain in the army.

**Graphic Organizer**
**Directions:** Compare the life of Meriwether Lewis to William Clark. Complete the Venn diagram below.

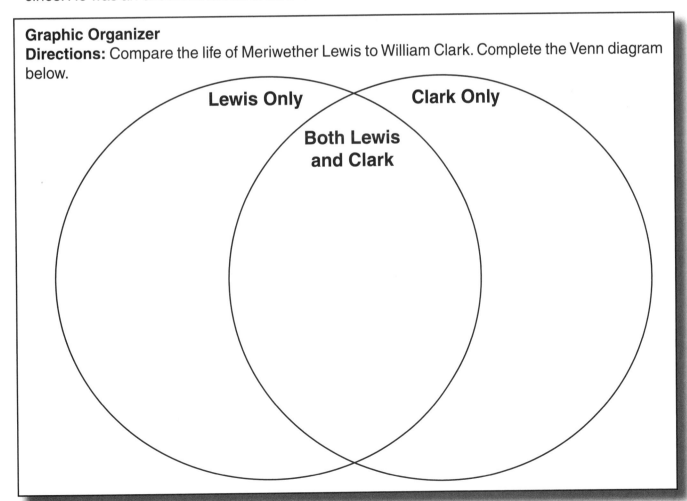

Name: _____ Date: _____

# Thomas Jefferson

UNIT ONE: LEWIS & CLARK

When Thomas Jefferson became the third president of the United States in 1801, he needed someone to become his personal secretary. Jefferson had known the Lewis family for a long time because they had been neighbors in Virginia. He decided to ask Meriwether Lewis to be his new secretary, and Lewis was pleased to accept the job.

At this time, the land to the west of the Mississippi River was largely unknown. Some white settlers called this land the **Great Unknown** or the **Back of Beyond**.

President Jefferson asked Lewis to lead an expedition through this land. What Jefferson wanted Lewis to find most of all was a water route from the Missouri River leading west to the Pacific Ocean. A water route would make it much easier to trade with China and other lands in the Far East. The only other way ships could trade with China was to sail all the way around South America and cross

the Pacific Ocean, and then the ships had to travel back again. This voyage would last from two to three years!

## Map

**Directions:** Look at the map at the right. Show the route a trading ship would take from the port of New Orleans to China and back. Use an atlas to help you label the Atlantic Ocean, the Gulf of Mexico, the Pacific Ocean, North America, Central America, and South America.

## Critical Thinking

What would be the advantage of a river route across America to the Pacific Ocean? Give specific details or examples to support your answer.

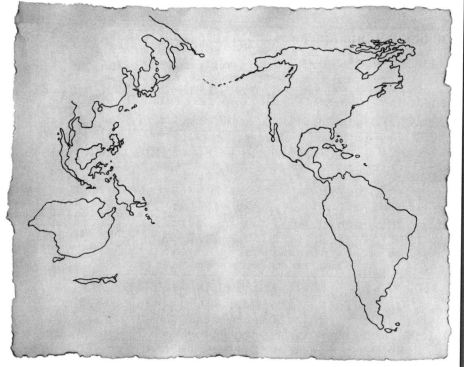

_____

_____

_____

_____

# The Louisiana Purchase

The land that President Jefferson wanted Lewis to explore did not belong to the United States. Although the land was the home of many Native Americans, Spain claimed this land as its own. It was known as the Louisiana Territory. For a time, Jefferson and Lewis kept their plans a secret. They did not want the Spanish to know that they were planning an expedition into Spanish territory.

Then, Napoleon Bonaparte of France forced Spain to give the Louisiana Territory to France in a secret treaty. Bonaparte, however, needed money for his war against Great Britain. He agreed to sell the entire Louisiana Territory to the United States for 15 million dollars. The Louisiana Purchase doubled the size of the United States. The purchase was also a great opportunity for President Jefferson—now the expedition would travel at least partly through American territory instead of Spanish territory.

The mountainous region beyond the Louisiana Territory was known as the Oregon Country. This land was the home of many Native Americans. Spain, Russia, and Great Britain all wanted a share of this area. President Jefferson also wanted this land for the United States. He thought he would be able to negotiate with the Native Americans after the expedition was over. He believed they could be persuaded to give up their land and their way of life. He thought they would not mind living among the white settlers as farmers.

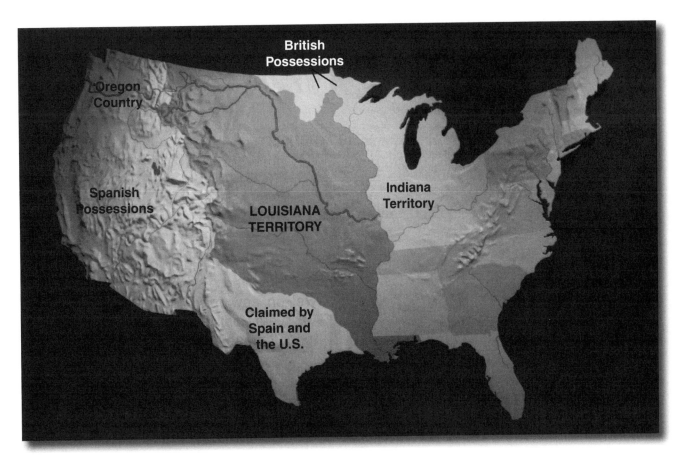

# The Louisiana Purchase (cont.)

**UNIT ONE: LEWIS & CLARK**

## Matching

_____ 1. Oregon Country

_____ 2. Napoleon Bonaparte

_____ 3. Louisiana Territory

_____ 4. President Jefferson

_____ 5. Louisiana Purchase

a. land claimed by Spain, but forced to give to France

b. doubled the size of the United States

c. wanted Lewis to explore the Louisiana Territory

d. mountainous region beyond the Louisiana Territory

e. agreed to sell the entire Louisiana Territory to the United States for 15 million dollars.

## Critical Thinking

What do you think about President Jefferson's idea that the Native Americans could be persuaded to give up their land and their way of life to become farmers? Write a paragraph explaining your ideas.

_____

_____

_____

_____

## Map

**Directions:** Use the map on the previous page to fill in the blanks below.

1. Use an atlas to determine which 15 modern states were at least partially formed from the Louisiana Purchase. List the states below.

_____   _____   _____

_____   _____   _____

_____   _____   _____

_____   _____   _____

_____   _____   _____

2. Which four states were formed from the Oregon Country?

_____   _____

_____   _____

# Preparing for the Journey

President Jefferson chose Lewis to lead the expedition. Lewis had five years of formal schooling. He was an amateur naturalist. He had studied medicine, botany, zoology, and celestial navigation. He had been a captain in the army.

President Jefferson wanted Lewis to do more than find a river route to the Pacific Ocean. He wanted him to draw accurate maps that included important landmarks and campsites, as well as latitude and longitude markings. Jefferson also wanted Lewis to record information about the climate, soil, plants, and animals.

In addition, he told him to make friends with the Native Americans and to find out about their languages, houses, religions, appearance, laws, and customs. He wanted to know what items they would like to trade or buy from the United States. He also wanted Lewis to keep a detailed journal of what happened on the expedition.

Lewis thought the expedition would have a better chance of success if it had a second leader. He decided to ask his friend William Clark to join him as a co-commander.

Clark was an experienced geographer, map maker, nature artist, and riverboat man. He had excellent hunting, fishing, trapping, and camping skills, and had also been a captain in the army.

Lewis had many tasks to do before he set out on the expedition. Some of these tasks included:

- Deciding the amount and kinds of supplies that would be needed
- Overseeing the construction of a custom keelboat
- Gathering medical supplies and scientific equipment
- Studying medicine, botany, zoology, and celestial observation
- Finding and buying supplies, including items for trade with Native Americans
- Recruiting crew members

The Lewis and Clark expedition used a custom-built, 55-foot **keelboat**, which could be sailed, rowed, poled like a raft, or towed from the riverbank. Two wooden row boats called **pirogues** were also used to hold men and supplies.

**Did You Know?**
To prepare for the trip, Lewis spent time with Andrew Ellicott, an astronomer, and Robert Patterson, a professor of mathematics. Patterson gave Lewis a formula to help him compute longitude through observations of the moon.

**Keelboat**

Name: _____ Date: _____

# Preparing for the Journey (cont.)

**Directions:** Read the partial list of supplies that Lewis and Clark took on the expedition and answer the questions below.

*List of Supplies*

| | | | |
|---|---|---|---|
| 1 | mariner's compass | 6 | copper kettles |
| 4 | tin blowing trumpets | 12 | gross fishing hooks |
| 24 | iron spoons | 2 | pick axes |
| 1 | microscope | | rope |
| 1 | tape measure | | nails |
| 6 | papers of ink powder | | spades |
| 4 | metal pens | | vises |
| 15 | rifles | | portable soup |
| 1 | lb. of ointment for blisters | | dried and salted rations |
| 2 | crayons | | mosquito curtains |
| 1 | pair of pocket pistols | | medicine |
| 30 | linen shirts | | scientific & mathematical equipment |
| | blankets, coats, socks | | knives |
| | air gun | | books about plants and animals |
| | cannons for the boats | | blacksmith tools |

1. Which items did you *not* expect to see on the above list? Explain, giving specific details to support your answer.

_____

_____

_____

2. Which items do you think would be important to take that are not on the above list? Explain, giving specific details to support your answer.

_____

_____

_____

3. What kinds of items would you take on an expedition today that were not available in 1804? Explain, giving specific details to support your answer.

_____

_____

_____

Name: _____ Date: _____

# Preparing for the Journey (cont.)

**Directions:** Read the list of items that Lewis and Clark took to trade with the Native Americans. Next, think about the Native Americans' point of view in 1804. Which items would be the most useful to them? Which items were decorative? Which kinds of items might they have already obtained from fur traders? Work with a partner to fill in the charts below. You may put an item in more than one category.

*Items for Trade*

| | |
|---|---|
| red silk handkerchiefs | eyeglasses |
| copper wire | glass beads |
| ribbons | tinsel tassels |
| brass buttons | burning glasses |
| fish hooks | small paper bells |
| jewelry | silver peace medals |
| blankets | knives |
| calico shirts | kettles |
| needles, thread, scissors, thimbles | hatchets |
| mirrors | tobacco |

| Useful Items | Decorative Items | Items Possibly Obtained from Fur Traders |
|---|---|---|
| _____ | _____ | _____ |
| _____ | _____ | _____ |
| _____ | _____ | _____ |
| _____ | _____ | _____ |
| _____ | _____ | _____ |
| _____ | _____ | _____ |
| _____ | _____ | _____ |
| _____ | _____ | _____ |

# The Lewis and Clark Expedition

## Part 1 of the Journey

After many delays, Lewis finally left Pittsburgh on August 31, 1803. His first task was to take his newly built keelboat down the Ohio River to Louisville, Kentucky. The trip was slow because the river was low and full of sandbars. Sometimes he and the soldiers who were with him had to unload the boat and lift it over the sand and rocks. They didn't reach Louisville until October 15, 1803.

Lewis met Clark and continued down the Ohio River to the Mississippi River. From there they had traveled up the Mississippi River to the Missouri River. They stopped for the winter and built Camp Wood, which was twenty miles north of St. Louis.

## Part 2 of the Journey

In the spring, the Corps of Discovery traveled west on the Missouri River from St. Louis. The river turned to the north where present-day Kansas City, Missouri, now stands. By July 21, the men had gone almost 600 miles and passed the mouth of the Platte River. The Corps continued north on the Missouri River. Lewis and Clark held their first council with the Oto near Council Bluffs, Iowa. Sergeant Charles Floyd died of appendicitis near

present-day Sioux City, Iowa. They had an unfriendly encounter with the Teton Sioux in South Dakota and then continued north to the Mandan villages near what is now Bismarck, North Dakota. They spent the winter there.

## Part 3 of the Journey

The Corps of Discovery then traveled west on the Missouri River from Fort Mandan. They took the southern fork of the Missouri River past Great Falls to Three Forks. They followed the western-most fork that they named the Jefferson River for a ways. From there, they traveled north by land through the Bitterroot Range of the Rocky Mountains to the Lolo Trail. Then they went west on the Lolo Trail through the Rocky Mountains. They traveled from the Clearwater River, to the Snake River, to the Columbia River, to the Pacific Ocean. They spent the winter at Fort Clatsop.

### Did You Know?

Lewis and Clark had the opportunity to name places and rivers on their journey. They named three forks in the Missouri River: the Jefferson, the Madison, and the Gallatin. Madison was the secretary of state, and Gallatin was the secretary of the treasury at the time. They named Slaughter Creek for the place where Native Americans had stampeded a buffalo herd off a cliff. They named Council Bluffs for the place they held the first council with Native Americans.

Name: _____ Date: _____

# The Lewis and Clark Expedition (cont.)

## Part 4 of the Journey

The expedition left Fort Clatsop on March 23, 1806. The Corps of Discovery headed up the Columbia River, but this time they had to travel against the current. By May 3, the expedition had reached the Nez Percé villages where they retrieved the horses they had left there the previous winter. With the help of several Nez Percé guides, they crossed the Lolo Trail in only six days.

From there, Lewis went north to explore the Marias River. He wanted to see if this river would be a water route up to Canada and its rich fur trade. The river, however, veered into the Rockies. After that, he had a serious clash with the Blackfeet tribe. Later, Lewis and his men were hunting elk when one of the men accidentally shot Lewis in the behind.

Clark's team took a different route. They went past Three Forks, then down the Yellowstone River to the Missouri. There his team met up with Lewis's team. The Mandan Chief Sheheke joined the explorers so he could visit President Jefferson. They returned to St. Louis by September 21, 1806; the journey home had only taken them six months.

**Technology in the Classroom**
**Primary Source:** <http://memory.loc.gov/cgi-bin/query/r?ammem/
mtj:@field(DOCID+@lit(je00062))>
("Meriwether Lewis to Thomas Jefferson, April 7, 1805, with Invoice," Library of American Memory)
**Primary Source:** <http://lewisandclarkjournals.unl.edu/>
("The Journals of the Lewis and Clark Expedition, edited by Gary Moulton," University of Nebraska Press)

**Directions:** Examine the two primary sources. Incomplete sentences and misspellings are a common mistake in the journal entries of William Clark. In 1805, Meriwether Lewis sent a portion of Clark's private journal to Thomas Jefferson from Fort Mandan. In his letter, Lewis states, "Capt. Clark does not wish this journal exposed in it's present state, but has no objection, that one or more copies of it be made by some confidential person under your direction, correcting it's grammatical errors &c." Using the April 1, 1805, journal entry by William Clark, rewrite the entry using correct grammar, sentence structure, and spelling.

Name: _____  Date: _____

# Clark's Journal

In the spring of 1804, the Corps of Discovery continued to travel west on the Missouri River. When they arrived at the place where Kansas City, Missouri, now stands, the river made a great bend to the north. Beyond this area, the men first saw the Great Plains.

Clark wrote in his journal about the grass, springs, brooks, shrubs covered in delicious fruit, and the scented flowers. The Great Plains teemed with wildlife. There were beavers in the streams and elk and deer in the woods. Buffalo herds roamed the plains.

Many of the animals were new to the members of the expedition. They had never before seen a badger, coyote, pronghorn, jackrabbit, mule deer, bull snake, or a magpie. Clark drew sketches of the animals, and Lewis described each one in his journal. They collected and preserved samples of plants and animals to send back to President Jefferson.

**Directions:** Learn more about one of the animals in the reading exercise above. On the journal page below, write a short description of this animal. Make a sketch of the animal next to your description.

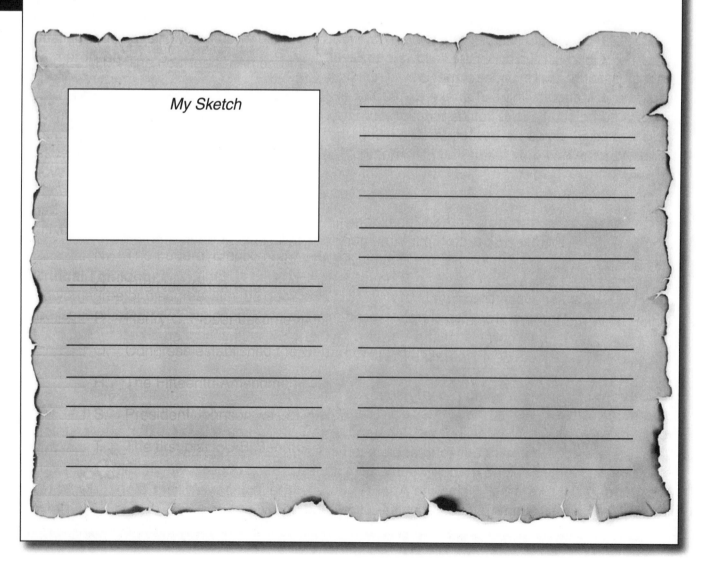

*My Sketch*

Name: _____ Date: _____

# The Teton Sioux

The Teton Sioux lived on both sides of the Missouri River in what is now South Dakota. They tried to control any trade between fur traders from St. Louis and other tribes that lived upstream. The Teton Sioux would allow fur traders to pass only after they had given the Sioux enough gifts.

The first group of Sioux arrived at the Corps of Discovery's camp in late September of 1804. They were not impressed by the corps' uniforms or by the air gun. They seized one of the expedition's pirogues and all its cargo. The situation became tense as the Sioux readied their bows with arrows, and the crew aimed their rifles. Then the chief, Black Buffalo, decided to return the pirogue and ask for peace.

The expedition still hoped to become friends with the Sioux, so they visited the Sioux village where there were about eighty tepees. There they ate dog meat and pemmican. The Sioux men and women performed dances for the explorers, but the situation remained tense. That night, the men moved their boats a mile up the river from the Sioux village. For the next three days, more Sioux began to arrive at the village. Finally, Black Buffalo allowed Lewis and Clark to leave in exchange for some tobacco.

The Lewis and Clark expedition did not succeed in making friends with the Sioux; however, both sides avoided any bloodshed, and the expedition continued up the Missouri River.

**Directions:** Number the events below in the order in which they occurred.

_____ A.    The Sioux seized one of the expedition's pirogues.

_____ B.    Black Buffalo allowed Lewis and Clark to leave after they gave him some tobacco.

_____ C.    The Sioux forced fur traders to give them gifts before they could continue upriver.

_____ D.    The Sioux were not impressed by the corps' uniforms or by the air gun.

_____ E.    The expedition first met the Sioux in late September of 1804.

_____ F.    Black Buffalo returned the pirogue.

_____ G.    For three days, more and more Sioux arrived at the village.

_____ H.    The Sioux readied their bows; the corps aimed their rifles.

_____ I.    The expedition visited the Sioux village.

_____ J.    The men moved their boats a mile up the river from the Sioux village.

Name: _____ Date: _____

# Winter at Fort Mandan

By October 1804, the expedition had traveled 1,600 miles from St. Louis up the Missouri River to the Mandan villages in what is now western North Dakota. The Mandans did not mind if the Corps wintered near them. The men built a small fort and named it Fort Mandan in honor of the Mandans.

The winter was bitterly cold. The men struggled to stay warm while the Mandans, wearing very few clothes, often played lacrosse on the frozen river. The men set up a blacksmith shop where they sharpened and repaired axes, hoes, and other metal tools for the Mandans. The Mandans paid them with corn for this service. During the winter, both the men and the Mandans hunted together for buffalo.

Almost every day, the Mandans or the Hidatsa, a neighboring tribe, visited the fort. They examined the keelboat and the blacksmith shop. They also were curious about York, who was William Clark's slave, since they had never seen a person of African-American heritage before. On New Year's Day, 16 men visited the Mandan village and danced for the Mandans. Lewis and Clark spent the winter writing detailed reports and making accurate maps for President Jefferson.

**Graphic Organizer**

**Directions:** Use the information in the reading exercise to compare and contrast how the men and Native Americans spent the winter at Fort Mandan. Fill in the charts below.

**How the Mandans Spent the Winter**

_____
_____
_____
_____
_____
_____
_____
_____

**How the Corps Spent the Winter**

_____
_____
_____
_____
_____
_____
_____
_____

Name: _____    Date: _____

# Sacajawea

Toussaint Charbonneau was a French-Canadian fur trader and interpreter. He was living among the Hidatsa tribe when Lewis and Clark first arrived at the Mandan villages. His young wife, Sacajawea, was a Shoshone native who had been captured by the Hidatsa. Her son, Jean Baptiste, was born in the spring. She called the baby "Pomp," which was Shoshone for "first born."

When the expedition left Fort Mandan, Charbonneau, Sacajawea, and Pomp traveled with them. Sacajawea helped gather native plants and saved valuable supplies from the river when some of the boats almost capsized. Later, she acted as the interpreter to bargain for horses from the Shoshone. Her presence with the expedition also assured native tribes that the Corps of Discovery was not a war party. The tribes all knew that a woman with a child would never accompany a war party.

UNIT ONE: LEWIS & CLARK

---

**Fill in the Blanks**

1. Toussaint Charbonneau was a French Canadian fur trader and _____.

2. Charbonneau, Sacajawea, and Pomp joined the expedition at _____ _____.

3. Sacajawea called her baby "Pomp," which was Shoshone for _____.

4. Sacajawea's presence with the expedition also assured native tribes that the Corps of Discovery was not a _____ _____.

5. Sacajawea was the wife of _____ _____.

**Graphic Organizer**

**Directions:** Complete the vocabulary chart by creating a definition, using the word in a sentence and drawing an illustration that helps you remember the meaning of the word.

| Word | Definition | Illustration |
|------|------------|--------------|
| **interpreter** | | |
| | Sentence | |

Name: _____    Date: _____

# Meeting the Shoshone

Lewis and a few men set out from Three Forks in August 1805 to look for the Shoshone tribe. He wanted to bargain with them for horses and a guide across the Rocky Mountains. He was worried because their food supplies were low, and it was hard to find game. The expedition needed to cross the mountains before winter began. The expedition's success and survival depended on finding the Shoshone.

The Shoshone were not well-armed; they feared the Hidatsa and the Blackfeet tribes that lived to the east and northeast. When Lewis finally met several Shoshone, they fled from him in fear. Eventually, he met three Shoshone women. With the help of George Drouillard, the expedition's sign language interpreter, he asked them to take him and his men to the Shoshone camp. They soon encountered 60 Shoshone who, along with their chief, Cameahwait, were going east to hunt buffalo. Lewis convinced them to come with him back to Three Forks to meet Clark and the others who were coming up the river with the canoes. When Sacajawea saw Cameahwait,

she realized he was her brother!

Sacajawea had been taken from the Shoshone five years earlier by the Hidatsa tribe. Toussaint Charbonneau, a French-Canadian trader, had bought her from the Hidatsa and made her one of his two wives; however, he did not treat her well.

It was hard work to translate from English to Shoshone. First, a question had to be asked in English, then translated into French, then translated into Shoshone. The answer had to be translated back from Shoshone to French to English.

---

**Directions:** Decode this message using the code below.

Z  I  V    D  V    M  L  G    W  I  Z  D  M    L  M  D  Z  I  W,    D  V

___ __ ___ _____ _____, __

U  V  D,    W  I  Z  D  M    L  M  D  Z  I  W    G  L    M  V  D    V  I  Z?

___, _____ _____ __ ___ ___?

Hint: Use the opposite letter

| A | B | C | D | E | F | G | H | I | J | K | L | M | N | O | P | Q | R | S | T | U | V | W | X | Y | Z |
|---|---|---|---|---|---|---|---|---|---|---|---|---|---|---|---|---|---|---|---|---|---|---|---|---|---|
| Z | Y | X | W | V | U | T | S | R | Q | P | O | N | M | L | K | J | I | H | G | F | E | D | C | B | A |

For the second step, write the message that you decoded *backwards* on the lines below.

___ __ ___ _____ _____, __

___, _____ _____ __ ___ ___?

Name: _____ Date: _____

# Mapping the Journey

Directions: Use an atlas to find the information needed to complete the map below.

1. Color the route the Lewis and Clark Expedition took red.
2. Label and indicate the locations of the Rocky Mountains. Use the following symbol to represent mountains. ⌃⌃⌃
3. Label the Ohio, Mississippi, Missouri, Columbia, Snake, and Clearwater Rivers.
4. Label the following cities: St. Louis and Kansas City in Missouri; Council Bluffs and Sioux City in Iowa; and Bismarck, North Dakota.
5. Label the Atlantic and Pacific Oceans.

Name: _____     Date: _____

# After the Expedition

Lewis arrived in Washington, D.C., in December, 1806, and Clark in January of 1807.

After the 28-month expedition, the privates and the sergeants received their pay. To reward a job well done, each one was given double pay. For the privates, that amounted to ten dollars per month. The sergeants received 16 dollars per month. Each man also received 320 acres of land. He also had the choice to remain in the army and pick his next place of duty or to receive an honorable discharge.

York received his freedom from William Clark. He returned to Louisville, Kentucky, and went into the freight-hauling business.

**Statue of York**

Charbonneau, who had been a civilian translator for the expedition, received $500 for his work, although he was, according to Lewis, "a man of no particular merit." He stayed at the Mandan villages with Sacajawea and Pomp. Pomp later went east, and Clark paid for his education.

Sacajawea may have died in 1812. However, some people believed she lived among the Shoshone in the Wind River Mountains of Wyoming until she was 94 years old.

Each captain received 1,600 acres of land and $1,228. Lewis became the Governor of the Upper Louisiana Territory. Clark became the Superintendent of Indian Affairs. He worked to protect tribal land rights.

Besides accomplishing its goals, the Lewis and Clark expedition enabled the United States to claim the Oregon region of North America. It opened the West to more fur trappers, mountain men, and others from the eastern part of the United States.

**Short Answer**

1. What was the total amount paid to each of the privates? _____

2. What was the total amount paid to each of the sergeants? _____

**Constructed Response**

1. Do you think granting his freedom was a good way to compensate York? Why or why not? Give specific details to support your answer.

   _____

   _____

   _____

2. Do you think Sacajawea should have been paid for her work? Why or why not? Give specific details to support your answer.

   _____

   _____

   _____

   _____

Name: _____ Date: _____

# Searching for Lewis and Clark

**Directions:** Find and circle these 30 words in the word search puzzle below. Words are printed forward, backward, horizontally, vertically, and diagonally in the puzzle.

| | | | | | |
|---|---|---|---|---|---|
| Lewis | Corps | York | Sacajawea | expedition | Clark |
| Pomp | keelboat | Missouri | pirogue | portage | Mandan |
| Columbia | Jefferson | buffalo | horses | natives | river |
| Three Forks | plains | Snake | Council Bluffs | Blackfeet | dugout |
| Shoshone | trade | Sioux | grizzly | Nez Percé | boats |

```
T  F  N  P  G  B  O  A  T  S  H  O  R  S  E  S  G  R
B  H  G  R  I  Z  Z  L  Y  Q  E  K  A  N  S  B  T  Z
M  H  R  M  K  Z  H  X  H  C  N  Y  G  N  U  B  E  F
E  C  R  E  P  Z  E  N  U  F  C  F  R  F  Q  S  E  K
Z  O  Q  A  E  M  V  K  B  O  E  R  F  L  R  I  F  X
M  U  C  E  R  F  R  T  R  D  I  A  B  H  P  W  K  K
I  N  K  W  K  M  O  P  A  D  L  S  K  M  K  E  C  E
S  C  S  A  H  L  S  R  U  O  Q  M  O  R  F  L  A  X
S  I  H  J  N  Y  T  G  K  R  D  P  Z  F  C  L  L  P
O  L  O  A  P  O  O  W  W  S  N  Q  N  L  K  L  B  E
U  B  S  C  P  U  S  R  W  C  O  L  U  M  B  I  A  D
R  L  H  A  T  O  N  R  K  N  E  B  L  T  W  L  S  I
I  U  O  S  C  A  R  R  E  U  A  M  K  R  Q  J  N  T
Z  F  N  R  T  L  Y  T  G  F  N  D  E  P  P  C  I  I
W  F  E  I  J  Y  A  O  A  T  F  V  N  W  X  R  A  O
Z  S  V  N  T  M  R  R  M  G  I  E  F  A  T  R  L  N
L  E  F  M  J  I  W  H  K  R  E  V  J  T  M  X  P  B
S  P  Z  P  P  T  N  Y  T  A  O  B  L  E  E  K  N  K
```

Name: _____ Date: _____

# Expedition Research Project

**Directions:** Learn more about the Lewis and Clark Expedition. Select one topic listed below for your research project. Construct a doorknob hanger to display your information. On the front, write your information, and on the back, include an illustration.

## People/Animals

Thomas Jefferson
Meriwether Lewis
William Clark
George Drouillard
York
Pierre Cruzatte
John Shields
John Ordway
Sacajawea
Seaman

## Equipment

Keelboat
Pirogues

## Places

Great Falls
Great Plains
Missouri River
Camp Wood
Fort Clatsop
Fort Mandan

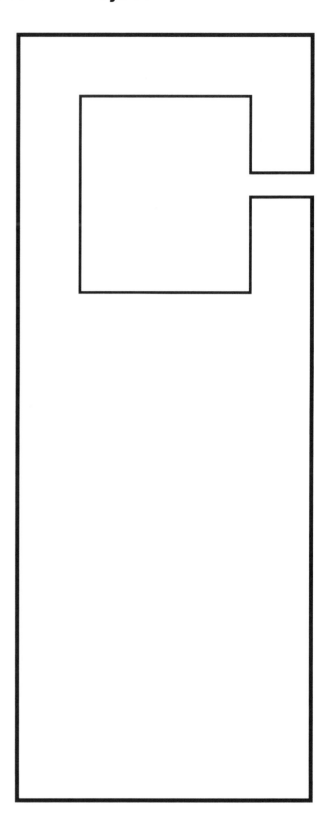

# Time Line of Westward Expansion and Migration

| | |
|---|---|
| 1783 | The Treaty of Paris established the Mississippi River as the western boundary of the United States. |
| 1789 | George Washington became the first U.S. President. |
| 1796 | John Adams elected president. |
| 1800 | The U.S. population reached five million. |
| | Thomas Jefferson elected president. |
| 1803 | The Louisiana Territory was purchased from France for $15 million, nearly doubling the size of the United States. |
| 1804 –<br>1806 | The Lewis and Clark Expedition explored the country for a water route to the Pacific Ocean. |
| 1805 | Lewis and Clark reached the Pacific Ocean. |
| 1806 | Zebulon Pike explored most of the American Southwest. |
| 1807 | John Colter explored the Yellowstone area. |
| 1808 | James Madison elected president. |
| 1807 | Meriwether Lewis became governor of the Louisiana Territory. |
| 1810 | Pacific Fur Company started by John Jacob Astor. |
| 1812 | The War of 1812 between the United States and Great Britain began. |
| 1816 | James Monroe elected president. |
| 1818 | The border between the United States and Canada established from the Lake of the Woods to the Rocky Mountains. |
| 1819 | Florida purchased from Spain. |
| 1821 | Mexico won independence from Spain. |
| 1823 | Stephen Austin established the first American settlement in Tejas (Texas). |
| 1824 | Jim Bridger became the first white man to see the Great Salt Lake. |
| 1826 | Jedediah Smith led the first party of Americans overland to California. |
| | Major George Sibley completed the first survey of the Santa Fe Trail. |
| 1827 | Dr. John McLoughlin built a lumber mill in the Pacific Northwest at Fort Vancouver. |
| 1828 | Andrew Jackson elected president. |
| 1830 | Joseph Smith established the Church of Jesus Christ of Latter-Day Saints. |
| | Congress passed the Indian Removal Act. |
| 1831–<br>1838 | The forced Indian removal from the East to Oklahoma occurred. This was later called the "Trail of Tears." |
| 1833 | Samuel Colt developed a revolver. |
| 1834 | Fort Laramie established. |
| 1835 | Texas war for independence from Mexico began. |
| 1836 | Sam Houston elected president of the Republic of Texas. |
| 1840 | William Henry Harrison elected president. |
| 1841 | John Bidwell organized the Western Emigration Society. |
| | William Henry Harrison died; John Tyler became president. |

UNIT TWO: WESTWARD EXPANSION & MIGRATION

# Time Line of Westward Expansion and Migration (cont.)

1842    Don Francisco Lopez discovered gold in the roots of an onion at Placeritas Canyon
            in the San Fernando Valley.

1843    Jim Bridger and Louis Vasquez established Fort Bridger.

            Free land in Oregon sparks "Oregon Fever."

            The "Great Migration": 1,000 pioneers left Independence, Missouri, on a 2,000-mile
            journey to the Willamette Valley.

1844    Mormon leader Joseph Smith killed; Brigham Young became the new Mormon leader.

            James K. Polk elected president.

            The first long distance telegram sent.

1846    Oregon Territory became a part of the United States.

            The Mormons were forced to leave Nauvoo, Illinois.

            The Mexican War began.

            The Donner Party met disaster.

1847    The Mormons established Salt Lake City.

1848    James Marshall discovered gold while building a lumber mill for John Sutter.

            Mexico ceded Arizona, California, Nevada, New Mexico, Utah, and western Colorado
            to the United States in return for $15 million after the Mexican War.

            Zachary Taylor elected president.

1849    The first ship carrying prospectors arrived in California. Wagon trains with approxi-
            mately 20,000 people headed for the Gold Rush. By the end of this year, 80,000
            people had arrived in California in search of gold.

1850    President Taylor died; Millard Fillmore became president.

1852    Franklin Pierce was elected president.

1853    The Gadsden Purchase was acquired from Mexico for $10 million.

1856    James Buchanan was elected president.

1860    The first Pony Express rider left St. Joseph, Missouri.

            Abraham Lincoln elected president.

1861    The Civil War began.

            Transcontinental telegraph service began.

1862    The Homestead Act was passed.

1865    President Lincoln assassinated; Andrew Johnson became president.

1867    Alaska purchased from Russia for $7.2 million in gold.

1868    Ulysses S. Grant elected president.

1869    The Transcontinental Railroad was completed.

            Major John Powell began exploration of the Colorado River.

1872    Yellowstone became the first national park.

            A railroad was completed to the Colorado border, ending the use of the Santa Fe Trail
            by most travelers.

Name: _____ Date: _____

# Westward Expansion and Migration Time Line Activity

**Directions:** Use information from the time line to answer the questions below. Place a check mark next to the event in each group that came first.

1. _____ Joseph Smith established the Church of Jesus Christ of Latter-day Saints.
   _____ Sam Houston was elected president of Texas.

2. _____ The War of 1812 began.
   _____ The United States purchased Florida from Spain.

3. _____ Louisiana Purchase
   _____ Treaty of Paris

4. _____ Trail of Tears
   _____ Mexico won independence from Spain.

5. _____ Congress passed the Indian Removal Act.
   _____ The United States purchased Alaska from Russia.

6. _____ Gold was discovered in California.
   _____ The Transcontinental Railroad was completed.

7. _____ The Pony Express began.
   _____ The Donner Party met disaster.

8. _____ The transcontinental telegraph was completed.
   _____ Yellowstone became the first national park.

9. _____ Brigham Young led the Mormons to Utah.
   _____ John Bidwell organized the Western Emigration Society.

10. _____ James Polk was elected president.
    _____ Abraham Lincoln was elected president.

11. _____ The Civil War began.
    _____ Abraham Lincoln was assassinated.

12. _____ Andrew Jackson was elected president.
    _____ The Oregon Territory became a part of the United States.

13. From what country did the United States gain Arizona, California, Nevada, New Mexico, and Utah? _____

14. Who established Fort Bridger? _____

15. Who became president when William Henry Harrison died in office? _____

# Westward Movement and Expansion

The westward movement across North America began shortly after the first colonies were established. Although most people settled along the coast or in port cities like Boston and New York, a few people were always a little bit braver, more adventurous, or more foolish than the rest.

By the time the French and Indian War ended in 1763, people had settled in much of the land as far west as the Appalachian Mountains. King George III tried to prevent further western colonization by issuing the Proclamation of 1763.

In 1769, Daniel Boone set out with five other men to explore the "western frontier," the area beyond the Allegheny Mountains through the Cumberland gap. During the next two years, he explored as far west as the present site of Louisville, Kentucky. The Transylvania Company hired Boone in 1769 to lead settlers to Kentucky. His trailblazing efforts established a new route used by thousands in the first major westward migration.

After the Revolutionary War, the Treaty of Paris (1783) set the Mississippi River as the western border of the United States, and "the West" meant all the way to the Mississippi River.

As the population of the original thirteen states grew and the economy developed, the desire to expand increased. For many Americans, land represented potential income, wealth, and freedom. Expansion in the western frontiers offered opportunities for self-advancement.

Each time people moved west and settled an area, "the West" moved farther west until it met the Pacific Ocean.

In 1803, President Thomas Jefferson purchased 831,321 square miles of land from Napoleon, the ruler of France, for $15 million. Known as the Louisiana Purchase,

the acquisition of this area nearly doubled the size of the United States, and the movement west gained momentum.

The Spanish were the first to explore and colonize Florida, but by 1815 the area had become a refuge for runaway slaves, buccaneers, and pirates. Many Americans thought Florida was part of the Louisiana Purchase. When settlers poured into the area, Spain objected.

When he was in his mid-60s, Daniel Boone left Kentucky to settle in Missouri. He claimed he was leaving Kentucky because it was "too crowded."

After two invasions in 1814 and 1818 by American troops, Spain decided to sell the area before it was taken by force. In the Treaty of 1819, Spain sold all land east of the Mississippi River and all claims to the Oregon Territory for $5 million. The United States also agreed to give up all claims to the part of Texas acquired in the Louisiana Purchase.

Name: _____ Date: _____

# Westward Movement and Expansion (cont.)

The United States acquired additional land from Great Britain in 1818, which established the border between Canada and the United States from the Lake of the Woods to the Rocky Mountains. This included a small part of South Dakota, parts of northern and western Minnesota, and the eastern and northern parts of North Dakota.

Territory north and west of the Louisiana Purchase (present-day Oregon, Washington, Idaho, and parts of Montana, Wyoming, and Canada) were claimed by both the United States and Great Britain. Both had established trading posts and settlements in the area.

Neither Britain nor the United States wanted to go to war over the issue and an agreement was finally reached in 1846. The United States received all land south of the 49th parallel except Vancouver Island.

**Fill in the Blanks**

1. King George III tried to prevent further western colonization by issuing the
   _____ of _____.

2. The Transylvania Company hired Boone in 1769 to lead settlers to
   _____.

3. For many Americans, land represented potential _____, _____, and _____.

4. The Spanish were the first to explore and colonize _____, but by 1815 the area had become a refuge for runaway slaves, buccaneers, and _____.

5. The United States acquired additional land from Great Britain in 1818, which established the border between _____ and the United States.

**Research**

**Directions:** Research the Proclamation of 1763. Why was it issued?

_____

_____

_____

_____

_____

_____

_____

_____

_____

_____

UNIT TWO: WESTWARD EXPANSION & MIGRATION

Name: _____ Date: _____

# Manifest Destiny

Once it became an independent nation, the United States experienced a rapid increase in population due to immigration and a high birthrate. Since agriculture was the basis for the economic structure of the country, large families to work the farms were an asset. The U.S. population grew from more than five million in 1800 to more than 23 million by mid-century.

This population explosion increased the need to expand into new territory. As parts of the Louisiana Territory became settled, ordinary Americans began walking, riding, and driving wagons over the immense mountains to reach the fertile farmlands of Oregon and California. Some historians estimate that nearly 4 million Americans moved to western territories between 1820 and 1850.

Americans believed that Manifest Destiny was both a right and an obligation. However, the rights of Native Americans who claimed the same land was ignored. Those who resisted were either forcibly removed or killed.

Frontier land was usually inexpensive, and sometimes was even free, promising a better life for those who didn't own land. Some people moved west simply because they desired adventure. The discovery of gold in California in 1848 and the completion of the Transcontinental Railroad in 1869 were other factors that attracted people to the West.

## Critical Thinking

In 1845, a New York editor wrote: *"It is America's 'Manifest Destiny' to overspread and to possess the whole of the continent which Providence has given us for the development of the great experiment of Liberty and federated self-government entrusted to us."*

**Directions:** Read the above quote. In your own words, explain what you think the New York editor meant. Give specific details and examples to support your opinion.

_____

_____

_____

_____

_____

_____

_____

_____

_____

_____

UNIT TWO: WESTWARD EXPANSION & MIGRATION

Name: _____ Date: _____

# Expanding Into the Southwest

After Mexico won independence from Spain, the lands once claimed by Spain became part of Mexico. This included the present states of Texas, California, Nevada, Utah, Arizona, and New Mexico, as well as parts of Colorado and Oklahoma.

Although the United States had agreed to give up claims to Texas in the Treaty of 1819, thousands of American ranchers, farmers, and adventurers settled in Texas. The Mexican government permitted Americans to establish settlements in their territory, if the settlers agreed to become Mexican citizens.

Disagreements arose between the Mexican government and the Texans. Finally, the Texans ratified their own constitution and declared Texas an independent republic in 1836.

After defeating the Mexican general Santa Anna and his troops in the war for independence, Sam Houston was elected president of the new **republic**.

In 1845, Texas was annexed by the United States, but there was a dispute over exactly where the border of Texas was. War between Mexico and the United States broke out a year later. To end the war, Mexico signed the Treaty of Guadalupe-Hidalgo, giving up claims to Texas and California, most of New Mexico and Arizona, all of Nevada and Utah, and parts of Idaho, Wyoming, and Colorado in exchange for $15 million paid by the United States.

In 1853, James Gadsden negotiated the purchase of the land south of the Gila River (southern Arizona and New Mexico) from Mexico for $10 million. This completed the acquisition of the land in the continental United States.

If Mexico had not lost the war, much of what is now the southwestern part of the United States would have remained a part of Mexico, making Mexico a far larger, more powerful country.

**UNIT TWO: WESTWARD EXPANSION & MIGRATION**

## Graphic Organizer

**Directions:** Complete the vocabulary chart by creating a definition, using the word in a sentence and drawing an illustration that helps you remember the meaning of the word.

| Word | Definition | Illustration |
|------|------------|--------------|
| **republic** | | |
| | Sentence | |

Name: _____ Date: _____

# Alaska and Hawaii

## Alaska

Even after gaining control from the Atlantic to the Pacific, the United States continued to grow. When the Czar of Russia agreed to sell Alaska for $7.2 million, Secretary of state William Seward jumped at the chance to acquire more territory.

Not everyone thought Alaska was a good buy. The purchase was nicknamed "Seward's Folly" by those who believed the purchase of "icebergs and walruses" was a waste of money. In 1959, Alaska became the 49th and largest state.

## Hawaii

By 1875, Hawaii had become a regular port of call for American ships in the Pacific. The U.S. had established friendly relations with the island government, and Americans gradually took control of the sugar industry. They also tried to control the government. When the Hawaiian royalty tried to regain control in 1893, Americans living there overthrew the government. They presented a treaty of annexation to the United States. President Cleveland refused the treaty, and the islands became a republic until 1898, when the Hawaiian islands became a U.S. territory. Hawaii became the 50th state in 1959.

Alaska: 586,412 square miles

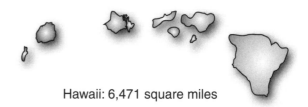

Hawaii: 6,471 square miles

## Graphic Organizer

**Directions:** Take a sheet of paper and make a hot dog fold. Cut the overlapping section into two flaps. On one flap, write the word **Alaska**. On the other, write **Hawaii**.

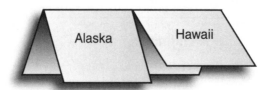

Research to learn more about the acquisitions of Alaska and Hawaii. Under the appropriate flap, describe the area, who lived there, what countries claimed part or all of the area, and how it eventually came to be part of the United States.

Name: _____ Date: _____

# Mountain Men

Novels and movies have portrayed mountain men as poor, unsociable, unwashed, and grizzled older men, wearing dirty clothing, and in need of a haircut. They were depicted as men who spent most of their lives hunting and trapping, far from civilization.

That image may have been true for a few mountain men in the early 1800s, but they were not all like that. Most mountain men went into the fur trapping and trading business to make money, and for a time, these men could earn large sums of money. Many were young men in their late teens or early twenties who became trappers and hunters for only a few years. Jim Bridger began his long, colorful career as a mountain man at the age of 17.

Mountain men probably didn't bathe often and wore dirty clothes, but few people at that time took baths or changed clothes very often. Did they have long, uncombed hair? They probably did, but so did a lot of other men at that time. Were they unsociable? Some might have been, but not all of them were. Many were married and had families. Many would travel in large groups to a central camp, and then each would set out in a different direction to set traplines.

**Jim Bridger**

Most surprising, not all mountain men were men! A few mountain women also made their livings trapping and hunting.

Not only were the mountain men a symbol of America's wild frontier, their role in westward expansion was also very important. They did not simply wander around the Great Plains and Rocky Mountains waiting for people to tell adventure stories and tall tales about their lives. They were explorers and guides who helped settle the land west of the Mississippi.

**Directions:** Research to learn more about the lives of one of these mountain men.

| | | | |
|---|---|---|---|
| Kit Carson | Jim Bridger | Jim Beckworth | Jedediah Smith |
| Thomas Fitzpatrick | Etienne Provost | Hugh Glass | |

Use your research to create a trading card. The front side should have a picture or illustration of the mountain man. On the reverse side of the card, write the name of your mountain man, date and place of birth, date and place of death, and at least five important facts about his life as a mountain man.

# Fur Traders Led the Way

Fur traders in the upper Missouri River area relied on Native Americans to bring bison hides to trading posts. From there the hides were sent down river to St. Louis. Manuel Lisa ran the Missouri Fur Company from about 1807 to 1820. This ad appeared in the *Missouri Gazette & Public Advertiser* on March 20, 1822.

> *TO ENTERPRISING YOUNG MEN: The subscriber wishes to engage ONE HUNDRED MEN, to ascend the River Missouri to its source, here to be employed for one, two, or three years. For particulars, enquire of Major Andrew Henry, near the Lead Mines, in the County of Washington, (who will ascend and command the party) or the subscriber, at St. Louis.*

The Rocky Mountain fur trading system was quite different. There, beaver was the fur of choice. Beaver hats were the fashion statement of the day in America and Europe. Beaver and other pelts were sold at an annual rendezvous where buyers and trappers met. The furs were taken by wagons to be sold in larger cities.

The first substantial American fur trading venture was the Pacific Fur Company, which was started by John Jacob Astor in 1810. An expedition by Astor overland laid the groundwork for the Oregon Trail by discovering the South Pass through the Rocky Mountains. This route was later one of the major overland routes to the West.

By 1834, there was little demand for beaver and few beavers left to trap. The fickleness of fashion now demanded hats of silk.

After the fur trade died, the mountain men became invaluable guides and scouts for wagon trains, survey teams, and the army. Their skills in living off the land and their knowledge of Native Americans helped bring many pioneers safely across the country.

**Directions:** Imagine you are looking for a guide for your wagon train. Write a help-wanted ad for the position and include the qualifications needed.

### HELP WANTED

_____
_____
_____
_____
_____
_____
_____

Name: _____ Date: _____

# Native Americans in the East

From the time the first European settlers began colonizing North America, there were conflicts with the Native Americans. What happened to the Narraganset, the Mohican, the Pokanoket, and other once-powerful groups of Native Americans? For two hundred years, the populations of those and other tribes dwindled in the East as whites pushed westward.

One of the few tribes to coexist with the whites for any length of time were the Cherokee living in northern Georgia. In 1828, when Andrew Jackson was elected president, gold was discovered at Dahlonega, Georgia. Gold fever swept the South, and the Cherokee people were attacked, their lands taken, and treaties broken.

When the Cherokee tried to use the legal system to protect their rights, the governor of Georgia stated, "Treaties were expedients by which ignorant, intractable, and savage people were induced without bloodshed to yield up what civilized peoples had a right to possess."

President Jackson was not sympathetic to Native Americans. When the Supreme Court ordered the federal government to protect the Cherokee nation from attack, Jackson refused to send help. He believed the Indian Removal Plan was the only solution to all conflicts between whites and Native Americans. This plan involved resettling all Native Americans who lived east of the Mississippi River on land west of the river.

Some members of the Cherokee Nation wanted to fight this plan in court. Others wanted to go to war. Some made plans to hide in caves in the hills. Others simply gave up and moved west.

Before the plan became a law, the state of Georgia organized a lottery to give away the Cherokee land to the winners.

**Technology in the Classroom**
**Primary Source:** <http://ourdocuments.gov/doc.php?flash=true&doc=25&page=transcript>
("Transcript of President Andrew Jackson's Message to Congress on Indian Removal (1830)." Ourdocuments.gov)

**Directions:** On December 6, 1830, President Andrew Jackson gave his annual message to Congress. He addressed the relocation of eastern Native Americans. In paragraph two, President Jackson stated, "The consequences of a speedy removal will be important to the United States, to individual States, and to the Indians themselves." Examine paragraph two of the primary source. Below, list Jackson's justifications for removal.

_____

_____

_____

_____

_____

_____

UNIT TWO: WESTWARD EXPANSION & MIGRATION

Name: _____ Date: _____

# The Trail of Tears

**Andrew Jackson**

Under Andrew Jackson, the Indian Removal Act became law. This affected all Native Americans east of the Mississippi, not only the Cherokee.

In the winter of 1831, the forced removal of the Choctaw began. The government had agreed to feed and clothe the people during their journey, but the money was never spent on provisions for them. Many were barefoot; most had no coats or blankets, yet they were forced to travel on foot across the frozen Mississippi River.

The Creeks were put in chains and forced from their homes in 1836 by U.S. soldiers. About 3,500 died of hunger and exposure before they reached their new territory. The following year, the Chickasaw were also forced to leave.

A long court battle delayed their removal but did not help the Cherokee. In 1838 their nightmare began. An army of 7,000 men dragged the people from their homes without warning and herded them into camps with nothing but the clothes they wore.

An estimated 17,000 Cherokee men, women, and children began their journey to Oklahoma on what came to be called the Trail of Tears. About 25 percent of those who started died along the way. It took nearly six months for those who lived to reach their destination.

**Tah-chee, a Cherokee Chief**

Of the five major tribes east of the Mississippi, only the Seminoles tried to fight. After a long, bloody war, they too were defeated and forced to move.

### Technology in the Classroom

**Primary Source:** <http://hdl.loc.gov/loc.rbc/rbpe.1740400a> ("Orders No. [25] Head Quarters, Eastern Division Cherokee Agency, Ten. May 17, 1838." The Library of Congress)

**Directions:** General Winfield Scott issued orders to the troops who would force-march the Native Americans to lands west of the Mississippi. These orders were to be "read at the head of each company." Examine the primary source. Using a soldier's perspective, write a personal reflection concerning the orders. To make it easier to read, you may choose to use the full-text transcript available on the website.

# Bison

When the pioneers traveled west, they encountered vast herds of bison. Between 30 million and 200 million bison once roamed the American plains. Although pioneers called them buffalo, the correct word is bison.

Bison can weigh up to 2,000 pounds and be more than 12 feet long and over 6 feet tall at the peak of the massive shoulder hump. More than 20,000 years ago, they **dominated** the American plains from the Mississippi River west to the Rocky Mountains.

---

**Think About It**

In his journal entry of September 17, 1804, Meriwether Lewis described seeing a herd of bison, ". . . immence herds of Buffaloe . . . I do not think I exagerate when I estimate the number of Buffaloe which could be compre[hend]ed at one view to amount to 3000."

---

Native Americans hunted bison for thousands of years, killing only what they needed and using every part of the animal for food, clothing, and tools. This hunting had little effect on the huge herds.

Travelers who crossed the Great Plains in the early 1800s often heard the rumbling of what sounded like thunder in the distance, even when the skies were clear. Suddenly, the ground would shake as a huge herd of bison thundered past. Those early settlers and the ones who followed were responsible for the near **extinction** of the bison.

First came trappers and fur traders, people who made their living selling meat and hides. As railroad and telegraph crews worked their way across the plains, hunters shot bison to provide food for the workers, often taking only the best meat and leaving the rest.

Later, train companies offered tourists the chance to shoot bison from the windows of their coaches. The animals they killed were left to rot in the sun.

People even held bison-killing contests to see who could kill the most animals in the shortest amount of time. Buffalo Bill Cody reportedly shot more than 4,000 bison in two years.

Some officials thought destroying bison herds would help **defeat** Native Americans who resisted the takeover of their lands by white settlers. James Throckmorton, a Congressman from Texas, stated, "It would be a great step forward in the civilization of the Indians and the **preservation** of peace on the border if there was not a buffalo in existence."

By 1880 bison were nearly extinct. Where millions of animals had once roamed, only a few thousand remained, and even that number continued to **decline**.

# Bison (cont.)

**Directions:** Complete the following activities.

## Matching

_____ 1. dominated
_____ 2. extinction
_____ 3. defeat
_____ 4. preservation
_____ 5. decline

a. the act of keeping something from becoming extinct
b. to overcome
c. control by being larger in number or quantity
d. to grow smaller
e. no longer exists

## Fill in the Blanks

1. Although pioneers called them _____, the correct word is bison.

2. Bison can weigh up to _____ pounds and be more than _____ feet long and over 6 feet tall at the peak of the massive shoulder hump.

3. First came _____ and _____ traders, people who made their living selling meat and hides.

4. Later, train companies offered _____ the chance to _____ bison from the windows of their coaches.

5. Some officials thought destroying bison herds would help defeat _____ _____ who resisted the takeover of their lands by white settlers.

## Critical Thinking

Do you think it is important to save animal species like the bison from extinction? Give details and examples to support your opinion.

_____
_____
_____
_____
_____
_____
_____
_____
_____

# Narcissa and Marcus Whitman

**Narcissa and Marcus Whitman**

From the time she was 16, Narcissa Prentice wanted to become a **missionary** to the Native Americans of the West. However, this wasn't allowed because she was a young, single woman.

In 1836, Narcissa met Marcus Whitman, a doctor and preacher, who shared her desire to bring Christianity to the Native Americans. They married and immediately made plans to move west with Henry and Eliza Spalding, another missionary couple.

The two couples traveled by stagecoach to St. Louis, and then took a steamboat up the Missouri River to Liberty, Missouri. There they purchased wagons, supplies, horses, mules, and cattle. They were accompanied on their journey west by a group of fur traders. Narcissa and Eliza became the first white women to cross the Rocky Mountains, several years before the first wagon train traveled west.

The group ran into trouble from the beginning, both from the weather and the **terrain**. Little by little, they abandoned their equipment as it broke or wore out.

The Spaldings decided to settle among the Nez Percé in Idaho, and the Whitmans went to live among the Cayuse in the Walla Walla Valley; there they built a **mission**. Marcus practiced medicine, Narcissa taught school, and they both preached the gospel.

Some critics felt the Whitmans were too rigid in their ways and made little effort to accommodate Cayuse practices and traditions. The Cayuse were not receptive to their sermons.

As more settlers traveled through the area, the Whitmans spent more time assisting settlers than ministering to the Cayuse. The growing number of settlers and the Whitmans' close association with them caused further **alienation** from the Cayuse.

When members of the Cayuse tribe caught **measles** from passing emigrants in 1847, more than half died, including most of their children. Convinced the sickness was a plot to kill them all, Chief Tiloukalt led a raid on the mission. The Cayuse killed Marcus, Narcissa, and 12 other settlers, and then they burned down the mission.

Retaliation by the militia nearly wiped out the entire tribe. The remaining members joined nearby tribes, and the Cayuse ceased to exist as an independent people.

Name: _____  Date: _____

# Narcissa and Marcus Whitman (cont.)

**Directions:** Complete the following activities.

## Matching

_____ 1. missionary

_____ 2. terrain

_____ 3. mission

_____ 4. alienation

_____ 5. measles

a. contagious viral disease

b. feeling of separation

c. physical features of a tract of land

d. someone who tries to convert someone else to their religious beliefs

e. houses an organized religion; like a church

## Fill in the Blanks

1. In 1836, Narcissa met Marcus Whitman, a _____ and _____, who shared her desire to bring Christianity to the Native Americans.

2. The Whitmans moved west with _____ and _____ Spalding, another missionary couple.

3. Narcissa and Eliza became the first white women to cross the _____ Mountains.

4. Marcus practiced _____, Narcissa taught _____, and they both preached the gospel.

5. The _____ killed Marcus, Narcissa, and 12 other settlers, and then they burned down the mission.

## Critical Thinking

From the Cayuse point of view, write a paragraph describing how you feel about the Whitmans. Give details and examples to support your opinion.

_____

_____

_____

_____

_____

_____

_____

_____

# Trails Led West

**Pioneers** who traveled west followed Native American trade routes and hunting **trails** that had been used for centuries. However, no Native American trail led all the way from Missouri to Santa Fe, California, or Oregon.

**Kit Carson**

By the late 1830s, mountain men and explorers like Kit Carson, Jim Bridger, Zebulon Pike, and Tom Fitzpatrick had explored most of the routes.

Beginning in 1840, people started moving west in large numbers. Members of the "Emigrant Societies" helped establish passable overland trails to the West and wrote guidebooks for travelers.

When people decided to join a wagon train and follow the Santa Fe or Oregon Trail, they had to leave many of their **possessions** behind. They knew they might never see their friends and relatives again. So why did people travel 2,000 miles or more to get to Oregon? Were they traveling *to* something or *away from* something?

Some went to take advantage of the free farmland available. Some hoped for a better life and a new start. Some searched for adventures and new experiences. Others wanted to escape problems at home.

When the pioneers traveled west, they knew there was little chance they would ever return. When people today move a long distance, they can return for visits. Most places in the United States can be reached by airplane in only a few hours. We also have other ways to keep in touch that weren't available to the pioneers.

The first wagon train, known as the Bidwell-Bartleson party, included 69 people who left Missouri in the spring of 1841. The group went as far as Soda Springs, Idaho; there they split up. Some went to Oregon and others to California.

Most trails to the west began at Independence or St. Joseph, Missouri, or Council Bluffs, Iowa. There were three major overland trails used by most people. Depending on their final destina-

**Zebulon Pike**

tion, most groups took either the Oregon Trail, the California Trail, or the Santa Fe Trail. Each trail had several variations.

Those traveling in wagon trains had to take routes that were not the most direct because of several natural obstacles: the canyons of Colorado, the Sierra Nevada Mountains, and the deserts around the Great Salt Lake.

Travelers faced many **obstacles** along the trails, including hills and mountains, streams and rivers, deserts, extremes of temperature, and hostile Native Americans who resented the **intrusion** into their lands.

---

### Did You Know?

Pioneers bound for Santa Fe had two choices. The Mountain Route followed the Arkansas River into Colorado before turning south. The Cimarron Cutoff crossed a waterless desert, but it saved about ten days travel.

CD-404138 © Mark Twain Media, Inc., Publishers

UNIT TWO: WESTWARD EXPANSION & MIGRATION

Name: _____    Date: _____

# Trails Led West (cont.)

**Directions:** Complete the following activities.

## Matching

_____ 1. pioneers

_____ 2. trails

_____ 3. possessions

_____ 4. obstacles

_____ 5. intrusion

a. paths

b. invade or enter without permission

c. settlers in a new territory

d. items you own

e. things blocking your path or plan of action

## Fill in the Blanks

1. Members of the "Emigrant Societies" helped establish passable overland trails to the West and wrote _____ for travelers.

2. No _____ _____ trail led all the way from Missouri to Santa Fe, California, or Oregon.

3. The first wagon train, known as the Bidwell-Bartleson party, included 69 people who left _____ in the spring of 1841.

4. Most trails to the west began at _____ or St. Joseph, Missouri, or _____ _____, Iowa.

5. Travelers faced many _____ along the trails.

## Critical Thinking

Who or what would you miss most if your family moved to another state? Why? Give specific details and examples to support your answer.

_____

_____

_____

_____

_____

_____

_____

_____

_____

Name: _____ Date: _____

# From Missouri to Santa Fe

Santa Fe was one of the first European settlements in what later became the United States.

The Santa Fe Trail was used regularly by traders beginning in 1821. The Osage tribe gave the U.S. government permission to use the Santa Fe Trail in 1825. The council where the right-of-way was granted was held under a tree, the Council Oak. For many years, Council Grove was the only trading post between Independence, Missouri, and Santa Fe, New Mexico.

From Independence, Missouri, to Santa Fe, New Mexico, the trail was about 780 miles long. Independence was founded in 1827. Five years later, it had become the center for supplies for wagon trans heading west and the beginning of both the Santa Fe and Oregon Trails for thousands of immigrants.

> **Did You Know?**
> The Santa Fe Trail was heavily used during the Mexican War to transport supplies for the army.

Settlers who followed the trail traveled west to the Arkansas River and then continued southwest along the river. The Santa Fe Trail offered two options. Travelers could continue along the river to Bent's Fort in Colorado and then head south through Raton Pass to Santa

Fe. The other route led across the Cimarron Desert.

The Cimarron Cutoff was shorter and easier for people traveling in covered wagons, but the risk of attack by Native Americans was higher, and water was scarce.

Merchant-traders traveled back and forth along the Santa Fe Trail with wagons or **mule trains**. Santa Fe was a major trading area where goods from Missouri could be exchanged for furs and other items.

Some people went to Santa Fe to make their homes and open businesses. Those who wanted to continue on could take either the Old Spanish Trail, which led to Los Angeles, or the El Camino Real, a trail south to Mexico City.

In 1880, the railroad reached Santa Fe, and use of the Santa Fe Trail declined.

## Graphic Organizer

**Directions:** Complete the vocabulary chart by creating a definition, using the word in a sentence and drawing an illustration that helps you remember the meaning of the word.

| Word | Definition | Illustration |
|---|---|---|
| **mule train** | | |
| | Sentence | |

Name: _____ Date: _____

# Santa Fe Trail

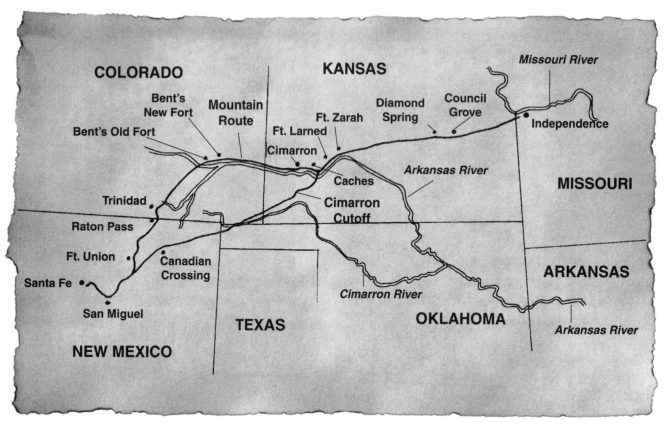

Name the state along the Santa Fe Trail where each place is located.

1. Bent's Old Fort _____

2. Bent's New Fort _____

3. San Miguel _____

4. Canadian Crossing _____

5. Caches _____

6. Fort Zarah _____

7. Independence _____

8. Trinidad _____

9. Council Grove _____

10. Diamond Spring _____

Name: _____ Date: _____

# Oregon Fever

In the 1820s, mountain men and fur trappers were the first to use the route that became the Oregon Trail. Missionaries began traveling to Oregon in the 1830s. Their letters home told of the fertile land, beautiful valleys, and gentle climate of Oregon, a land where anyone who farmed would prosper.

In 1843, a provisional government drafted Oregon's first constitution called the Organic Act and established laws for claiming land. Married couples could claim up to 640 acres at no cost if they cultivated the land and lived on it for four years. Half of the land would be in the woman's name, a change from laws in most states where women were not allowed to own property.

When word of free land spread east, thousands were infected with "Oregon Fever," a burning desire to own and farm fertile farmland. Land was the single most important reason why people undertook the long, difficult journey along the Oregon Trail. The first large wagon train set off for Oregon in 1843 led by Jesse Applegate. The train included 120 wagons, 1,000 people, 5,000 cattle, plus chickens, pigs, and dogs.

After 1850, the amount of free land available per couple was reduced to 320 acres. A single person could claim 160 acres. In 1854, the price of land was set at $1.25 an acre, with a limit of 320 acres for any one claim.

The Homestead Act of 1862 allowed the head of a family or single person over 21 to claim 160 acres of public land by paying a $34 fee if they lived on it and cultivated it for five years.

---

**True or False**

**Directions:** Circle "T" for true or "F" for False.

1. T  F    Oregon Fever was a disease many people caught after they arrived in Oregon.

2. T  F    The cost of 320 acres of land in 1854 was $400.

3. T  F    Women in every state were allowed to own property.

4. T  F    Missionaries were the first to travel the Oregon Trail.

5. T  F    In 1843, the law allowed married couples to claim up to 1,640 acres of free land.

6. T  F    Today, anyone willing to travel from Missouri to Oregon by wagon train can still claim free land.

7. T  F    The Organic Act stated that no pesticides could be used on farmland in Oregon.

Name: _____   Date: _____

# From Missouri to Oregon

Parts of the Oregon Trail had been blazed by Canadian explorers and the Lewis and Clark Expedition. Later, mountain men like Jim Bridger contributed their knowledge of the route and often acted as guides for groups heading west.

The Oregon Trail was the route pioneers took from Independence, Missouri, to the Columbia River in Oregon. At first, Oregon City was their destination. Later, settlers continued south to the fertile land of the Willamette Valley.

Part of the route followed the Platte River for about 540 miles through Nebraska to Fort Laramie. The trail continued along the North Platte and Sweetwater Rivers to South Pass.

From there, settlers traveled south to Fort Bridger, Wyoming, before turning into the Bear River Valley. There they headed north to Fort Hall in Idaho.

Once in Oregon, settlers passed through the Rhonda River Valley, crossed another mountain range, and then continued on to the Columbia River.

> **Did You Know?**
>
> In 1852, at the age of 23, Ezra Meeker made his first wagon journey on the Oregon Trail. In 1906, at the age of 76, Meeker loaded up a wagon, hitched two oxen, and made the trip again. Meeker enjoyed the trip so much that he did it again in 1910, and by automobile in 1916. In 1924, he flew over the trail in an open-cockpit army plane!

### Technology in the Classroom

**Primary Source:** <http://lib.utexas.edu/maps/historical/oregontrail_1907.jpg> ("Line of Original Emigration to the Pacific Northwest commonly Known as the Oregon Trail." The University of Texas at Austin)

**Directions:** The trip on the Oregon Trail was not easy. Settlers were faced with many natural obstacles. Some of these obstacles included rivers, endless flatlands, deserts, and mountains. Examine the primary source to learn more about the actual topography of the trail. Using salt-and-flour dough, create a three-dimensional trail map. A recipe for the salt-and-flour dough is listed below.

### Recipe: Salt-and-Flour Dough

2 cups flour   1/2 cup water
1 cup salt

Mix together the flour and salt. Add the water. If the dough is too sticky, add more flour/salt mixture. If too stiff, add more water. Knead the dough for 10 minutes until smooth. To color part of the dough, add colored powder drink mix.

Name: _____ Date: _____

# Oregon Trail

According to an official government survey, the main branch of the Oregon Trail from Independence, Missouri, to Oregon City, Oregon, was 1,930 miles long. Between 1840 and 1860, about 53,000 settlers traveled the Oregon Trail. There were many cutoffs and alternate routes along the way that people sometimes took. Some routes were shorter, but they were often more dangerous.

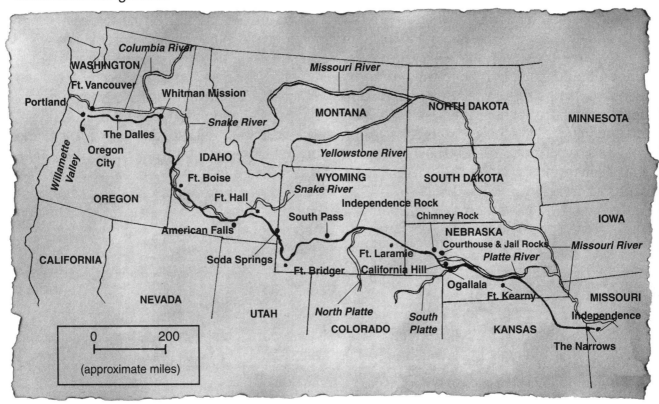

Name the state along the Oregon Trail where each place is located.

1. Fort Bridger _____

2. Willamette Valley _____

3. Ogallala _____

4. Chimney Rock _____

5. Fort Laramie _____

6. Fort Hall _____

7. Fort Kearny _____

8. South Pass _____

9. Independence _____

10. American Falls _____

11. Soda Springs _____

12. Oregon City _____

Name: _____  Date: _____

# Forts Along the Trails

Many forts along the Oregon and Santa Fe Trails were under the control of the U.S. Army. They housed soldiers who were stationed along the trails to keep peace with the Native Americans and protect travelers. However, some forts were owned by trading companies.

Forts provided places for travelers to rest, buy or trade for supplies, and to get equipment repaired. Prices for goods were usually much higher at forts than they were at the beginning of the trails.

Although the area enclosed by a fort was like a small community, the buildings were far from elegant. The buildings at Fort Bridger, built in 1843 by mountain man Jim Bridger, were "log cabins, rudely constructed,"

according to immigrant Edwin Bryant. Another traveler, Joel Palmer, described it as "… built of poles dabbed with mud."

Most forts were square or rectangular areas enclosed by strong wooden walls. Inside the walls were barracks for the soldiers, homes for the officers, offices, kitchens, bakeries, and mess halls. There were stables and grazing areas for the animals, vegetable gardens, and of course, latrines, since there was no indoor plumbing. Every fort needed a source of water—usually a well—for drinking, bathing, and doing laundry.

Some forts included buildings for carpenters, barbers, blacksmiths, dentists, or doctors. Some type of general store or trading center could also be found at most forts.

## Research

**Directions**: Research the following forts to see if they were located on the Oregon Trial or the Santa Fe Trail. Place the matching name of the trail on the line next to the name of the fort.

1. Fort Zarah _____

2. Fort Kearny _____

3. Fort Union _____

4. Fort Larned _____

5. Fort Vancouver _____

6. Fort Boise _____

7. Fort Bridger _____

8. Bent's Old Fort _____

9. Fort Hall _____

10. Fort Laramie _____

Name: _____ Date: _____

# Ride 'em, Cowboy!

Stories of the cowboys of the American West have long been popular in novels, movies, and on television. Most cowboys are pictured as white men, brave and self-reliant individuals.

Cowboys came to the West from all over the world. Many were Southerners, and some were from the Northeast. Some were Mexican, some European and Asian. About one in seven was African-American; in Canada, cowboys were as common as in the United States.

Their work was difficult and often monotonous, and they were usually poorly paid. The era of the cowboy matched the years of the great cattle boom (1866 to 1887), when huge herds of cattle were driven along trails to market.

Two of the most important items a cowboy owned were his horse and saddle. A good horse could make his job easier and, in an emergency, save a cowboy's life.

Since he spent as much as 16 hours a day in the saddle, it was important that a cowboy's saddle be comfortable. Rifles, pistols, ropes, and knives were also considered essential equipment for hunting and protection. Even the clothing cowboys wore served many useful, practical purposes.

**Technology in the Classroom**

**Primary Source:** <http://photoswest.org/cgi-bin/imager?10021563+X-21563> ("Black Cowboy and Horse." Denver Public Library Western History Photos Database)

**Directions:** Texas ranchers hired men for one dollar a day to drive herds to market in Kansas. Most cowboys were young men in their teens and early twenties. It was not uncommon to see African-American, Hispanic, and American Indian cowboys on the trail. Dust, heat, injuries, rustlers, and stampedes forced the young men to work together as a team to survive. Examine the primary source and research cowboy life. Using the information, write a letter home. From the perspective of a young cowboy, describe hardships and experiences you encountered driving cattle along the trail.

UNIT TWO: WESTWARD EXPANSION & MIGRATION

# Conestoga Wagons

What if you lived in the 1860s and your parents decided your family was going to move from Pennsylvania to Oregon? You know the trip will probably take about six months. For the journey, you will travel in a large, sturdy wagon with high sides called a **Conestoga**. Your top speed will be 15 to 20 miles a day.

People traveled in many types of wagons, but the Conestoga was considered the best and was the most expensive. They used horses, mules, or oxen to pull the wagons. Conestoga wagons were originally developed for hauling freight on the east coast. They were sturdy, well-built wagons suitable for traveling along the Santa Fe or Oregon Trail.

Conestogas were nicknamed "**prairie schooners**" because their high, white canvas tops looked like sailing ships as they crossed the sea of grass on the American prairie. The strong, broad wheels allowed the wagons to cross rutted roads, muddy flats, and the non-roads of the prairie. The curved floor was designed to reduce load shifting. Conestogas were capable of carrying loads up to six tons!

Some of the wagons had a convenience called a "flapp-a-doodle"—a box with shelves for food and cooking utensils—bolted to the rear of the wagons. The back of the box was a hinged door with wooden legs. When the door was lowered, the legs swung down, and the door became a table. The "flapp-a-doodle" was a combination kitchen table and cupboard.

Besides Conestogas, settlers also used common farm wagons with canvas tops supported by wooden arches. Although not as sturdy as Conestogas, these wagons were lighter and easier to pull.

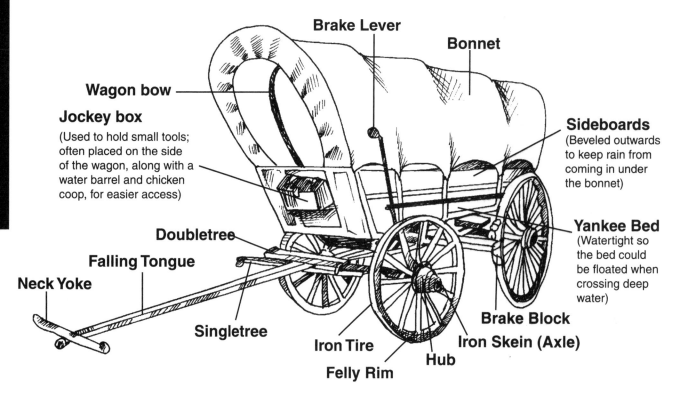

**Brake Lever**

**Bonnet**

**Wagon bow**

**Jockey box**
(Used to hold small tools; often placed on the side of the wagon, along with a water barrel and chicken coop, for easier access)

**Sideboards**
(Beveled outwards to keep rain from coming in under the bonnet)

**Doubletree**

**Falling Tongue**

**Neck Yoke**

**Singletree**

**Iron Tire**

**Felly Rim**

**Hub**

**Brake Block**

**Iron Skein (Axle)**

**Yankee Bed**
(Watertight so the bed could be floated when crossing deep water)

Name: _____  Date: _____

# Conestoga Wagons (cont.)

**Directions:** Complete the following activities.

**Fill in the Blanks**

1. A large, sturdy wagon with high sides was called a _____.
2. The top speed was _____ to _____ miles a day.
3. The Conestoga was considered the best and was the most _____.
4. Conestogas were nicknamed "_____ _____" because their high, white canvas tops looked like sailing ships.
5. The strong, broad _____ allowed the wagons to cross rutted roads, muddy flats, and the non-roads of the prairie.
6. Conestogas were capable of carrying loads up to _____ tons!
7. The "flapp-a-doodle" was a combination kitchen _____ and _____.
8. Besides Conestogas, settlers also used common _____ wagons with canvas tops supported by wooden arches

**Constructed Response**

Study the diagram on the preceding page. What was the purpose of the jockey box?

_____
_____
_____
_____
_____

**Activity**

**Directions:** Write a slogan or jingle a salesperson of Conestoga wagons might have used.

**Example:**   If you plan to travel west,

Conestogas are the best.

_____
_____
_____

# Supplying the Wagons

The pioneers couldn't stop at malls or convenience stores along the way. Although some places along the trail did carry supplies, the prices were higher and the availability of items was uncertain.

The typical covered wagon was four feet across and ten to 12 feet long. Much of that space was filled with food. Because of the amount of energy used, people needed nearly twice the amount of food per day they would normally eat. The following is what was recommended for one adult to make the journey to Oregon.

200 lbs. flour
10 lbs. rice
25 lbs. sugar
30 lbs. flat cracker-like bread
10 lbs. salt
 5 lbs. coffee
 $\frac{1}{2}$ bushel dried beans
75 lbs. bacon
 2 lbs. baking soda
 1 bushel dried fruit
 $\frac{1}{2}$ bushel cornmeal

Pioneers took cattle and other livestock with them. They could make butter from cow's milk and get eggs from chickens.

Berries or edible roots could be gathered along the way. Hunters sometimes found small game and occasionally shot larger animals, like bison or deer. When they were desperate, they ate snakes and prairie dogs. For the most part, the pioneers ate biscuits and beans, three times a day, day after day after day!

### Did You Know?

Making butter was one of the few easy tasks for pioneers on the trail. They put cream in a covered pail and hung it on the wagon. After a day on the trail, the constant jostling of the wagon turned the cream to butter.

UNIT TWO: WESTWARD EXPANSION & MIGRATION

Name: _____  Date: _____

# Supplying the Wagons (cont.)

The cost of supplies varied from month to month and town to town. These prices would have been typical in Missouri in the 1840s and 1850s.

| ITEM | PRICE | ITEM | PRICE |
|------|-------|------|-------|
| ox | $30–35 | milk cow | $70–75 |
| mule | $10–15 | horse | $25–75 |
| nails | $0.07/lb. | soap | $0.15/lb. |
| coffee pot | $0.75 | candles | $0.15/lb. |
| washtub | $1.25 | rifle | $15 |
| shotgun | $10 | hunting knife | $1 |
| flour | $0.02/lb. | cornmeal | $0.05/lb. |
| bacon | $0.05/lb. | sugar | $0.04/lb. |
| coffee | $0.10/lb. | salt | $0.06/lb. |
| pepper | $0.08/lb. | vinegar | $0.25/gal. |
| tea | $0.60/lb. | rice | $0.05/lb. |
| beans | $0.06/pound | dried fruit | $0.06/lb. |

1. Four to six oxen were needed to pull a heavy wagon. What is the least it would have cost for six oxen? _____

2. Which would have cost more: four oxen or eight mules? _____

3. How much would it have cost to buy a coffee pot, a washtub, ten pounds of soap, ten pounds of candles, a rifle, and a hunting knife? _____

4. How much would it have cost for 75 pounds of bacon, 25 pounds of sugar, five pounds of coffee, ten pounds of salt, and ten pounds of rice? _____

5. Which cost more: ten pounds of beans or two gallons of vinegar? _____

6. How much more per pound did tea cost than coffee? _____

7. In Oregon, nails sold for 17 cents a pound. Why do you think nails were more expensive in Oregon than in Missouri? _____

8. Compare the prices of any three food items then and now.

| Item | Cost Then | Cost Now | Difference |
|------|-----------|----------|------------|
|  |  |  |  |
|  |  |  |  |
|  |  |  |  |

# Wagon Trains

Rather than facing the perils of a long journey alone, most people who traveled west joined a wagon train—a group of ten or more wagons with 50 or more people led by a guide. During the journey, the people in a wagon train were like a small community. They elected leaders and made their own laws.

Most wagon trains left in early May. Timing was critical for the long journey. If they left too early in the year, there might not be enough grass to feed the animals along the way, and the ground might be too **soggy**. If they left too late, summer **drought** may have killed the grass before they could cross the prairie. They could encounter **blizzards** by the time they tried to cross the mountains.

Water was critical for people and animals, but not much could be carried because of the weight. Finding water along the way could make the difference between life and death.

When a family joined a wagon train heading west, they knew they were undertaking a long, dangerous journey. For a time, their wagons became their homes. Since the wagons were packed from top to bottom with supplies, there was very little living space. Many travelers slept under their wagons unless it was too wet or cold.

As the groups traveled west, wagon trains stretched out for a half-mile or more. The best position for a wagon was near the front of the **column**. Those in the rear had to "eat dust" all day long. In most wagon trains, people changed places in line each day.

On the trail, the day began before dawn. Even though there were chores to do, breakfast to make and eat, and animals to feed, water,

and harness, the travelers needed to leave early to travel as many miles as possible while there was still daylight. Wagon trains averaged 12 to 15 miles a day, depending on the terrain, the weather, and other factors.

Each wagon had to be in its assigned place when the leader gave the command to start. He might blow a bugle or shout the words, "Wagons, ho!" Those not ready to leave on time lost their assigned places and went to the back of the line.

Being at the front of the wagon train was an advantage because it was less dusty, but it also meant those who were first in line had to be ready to roll earlier than the others.

Wagon trains halted before dark. They turned the wagons to form a tight ring called a "night circle" as protection against attack. Men took turns as **sentries** around the outside of the circle.

Inside the circle people cooked, washed clothes, took care of their animals, made repairs to their wagons, and visited with each other. Besides being a form of protection, the night circle also gave the people on the wagon train a sense of community.

Name: _____ Date: _____

# Wagon Trains (cont.)

**Directions:** Complete the following activities.

## Matching

_____ 1. soggy

_____ 2. drought

_____ 3. blizzard

_____ 4. column

_____ 5. sentries

    a. severe snowstorm

    b. guards

    c. saturated with water

    d. period of time without needed rainfall

    e. straight line

## Fill in the Blanks

1. Rather than facing the perils of a long journey alone, most people who traveled west joined a _____ _____—a group of ten or more wagons with _____ or more people led by a guide.

2. They elected _____ and made their own _____.

3. Water was critical for people and animals, but not much could be carried because of the _____.

4. Since the wagons were packed from top to bottom with _____, there was very little living space.

5. On the trail, the day began before _____.

## Constructed Response

What were some advantages of being at the front of the wagon train? Disadvantages? Give specific details and examples to support your answer.

_____

_____

_____

## Critical Thinking

Explain what "a sense of community" means to you. Why would it have been important to those traveling with a wagon train? Give specific details and examples to support your answer.

_____

_____

_____

_____

UNIT TWO: WESTWARD EXPANSION & MIGRATION

Name: _____  Date: _____

# What Is It?

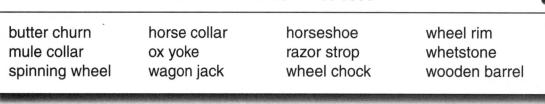

Use reference sources to identify each item pioneers may have taken with them on their journey to the west. Briefly explain what the item was used for.

**Example:**     Butter churn: Used to make butter.

Use the words in the box as clues. Not all words will be used.

| | | | |
|---|---|---|---|
| butter churn | horse collar | horseshoe | wheel rim |
| mule collar | ox yoke | razor strop | whetstone |
| spinning wheel | wagon jack | wheel chock | wooden barrel |

1. _____
   _____

2. _____
   _____

3. _____
   _____

4. _____
   _____

5. _____
   _____

6. _____
   _____

7. _____
   _____

8. _____
   _____

1.

2.      3.

4.      5.

6.

7.

8.

UNIT TWO: WESTWARD EXPANSION & MIGRATION

Name: _____ Date: _____

# Take It or Leave It?

Pioneers had to make many difficult decisions along the trail. Sometimes they had to abandon items they had brought from home. The decisions on what to take and what to abandon could be very difficult, but they could also be a matter of life or death.

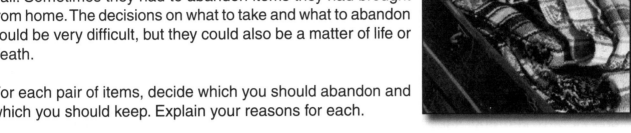

For each pair of items, decide which you should abandon and which you should keep. Explain your reasons for each.

1.  An empty water barrel or a beautiful dresser your grandfather made for you when you were a child?

    Abandon _____ because _____.

    Keep      _____ because _____.

2.  A keg of nails for building your new home or a barrel of flour?

    Abandon _____ because _____.

    Keep      _____ because _____.

3.  A spinning wheel or two barrels of salt pork?

    Abandon _____ because _____.

    Keep      _____ because _____.

4.  A cookstove or the baby's cradle?

    Abandon _____ because _____.

    Keep      _____ because _____.

5.  A barrel of flour or a box of school books?

    Abandon _____ because _____.

    Keep      _____ because _____.

6.  A beautiful wooden trunk filled with blankets and quilts or a hand-carved maple headboard and bedframe?

    Abandon _____ because _____.

    Keep      _____ because _____.

# Children On the Trail

Most children traveled the Oregon or Santa Fe Trail with their families. When parents died along the trail, children were usually adopted by another family and continued the journey.

At times, **orphans** might be left with families at forts, missions, or small settlements along the way. **Migrants** heading west on the Oregon Trail reportedly had an average of 3.4 children with them.

Although they didn't attend school while on the trail, the four-and-a-half to six-month journey was far from a vacation. Many children kept a diary or read the Bible to practice their reading and writing skills.

Except during very bad weather, only the very sick, very young, or very old rode in covered wagons. Many children walked a good part of the journey to lighten the load for the animals.

Riding in a wagon wasn't very comfortable, and children found that walking helped keep them from being bored. As they walked, they searched for berries and other **edible** plants and picked up firewood or bison chips

for fuel. Dried **bison chips** burned much more quickly than wood. It took two to three bushels of bison chips to cook a meal.

Even very young children had chores to do. The older the child, the more work was expected. Chores included **tending** the livestock, fetching water, taking care of younger children, helping with the cooking, washing clothes, and fishing.

Most children were so busy with chores and traveling that they had little time to play. However, they did participate in singing and dancing at night around the campfire, visited friends, and played games like Leapfrog, Hide the Thimble, and Crack-the-Whip.

Also, they made up games they could play with whatever material was available. They could draw a game board in the dirt with a stick and use whatever was handy for playing pieces, like small stones or wood chips.

They could skip stones across a river, hold running and jumping contests, or play hide-and-seek. Girls made dolls out of rags and corn husks. Children could also make up word games and rhyme games.

> ### Did You Know?
> Imagine being among the older children on a wagon train. One evening a week, you are expected to take your turn keeping the younger ones occupied for two hours while the adults prepare supper and do chores. You are responsible for 15 children between the ages of five and ten.

Name: _____ Date: _____

# Children On the Trail (cont.)

**Directions:** Complete the following activities.

## Matching

_____ 1. orphans

_____ 2. migrants

_____ 3. edible

_____ 4. tending

_____ 5. bison chips

a. those who move from one location to another

b. something you can eat

c. to take care of something

d. children whose parents have died

e. dried animal dung burned as fuel

## Fill in the Blanks

1. When parents died along the trail, children were usually _____ by another family and continued the journey.

2. Many children kept a diary or read the _____ to practice their reading and writing skills.

3. Many children walked a good part of the journey to _____ the load for the animals.

4. As they walked, they searched for berries and other edible _____ and picked up firewood or _____ chips for fuel.

5. It took two to three _____ of bison chips to cook a meal.

## Critical Thinking

What kinds of games could you and your friends play without fancy toys and equipment? Give specific details and examples to support your answer.

_____

_____

_____

_____

_____

_____

_____

UNIT TWO: WESTWARD EXPANSION & MIGRATION

# Journal of a Pioneer

John Bidwell, a member of the first wagon train to head west in 1841, wrote an account of the six-month journey from Missouri.

"The party consisted of sixty-nine, including men, women, and children. We had no cows ... and the lack of milk was a great deprivation to the children. My gun was an old flint-lock rifle, but a good one."

When the group was ready to start, they realized that "... no one knew where to go, even the captain ... We knew only that California lay west, and that was the extent of our knowledge."

When their guide joined them, the group set out for Idaho. "For a time, until we reached the Platte River, one day was much like another ... We had to make the road [as we went], frequently digging down steep banks, filling gulches, removing stones, etc."

"One of our men who chanced to be out hunting ... suddenly appeared without mule, gun, or pistol, and lacking most of his clothes, and in great excitement reported that he had been surrounded by thousands of Indians."

The "thousands of Indians" turned out to be a party of about 40 Cheyennes, "who did not intend to hurt the man or take his mule or gun, but that he was so excited when he saw them that they had to disarm him to keep him from shooting them."

"On the Platte River ... we had a taste of a cyclone; first came a terrific shower, followed by a fall of hail to the depth of four inches, some of the stones being as large as turkeys' eggs; and the next day a waterspout—an angry, huge, whirling cloud column ... passed ... behind us. We stopped and braced ourselves against our wagons to keep them from being overturned. Had it struck us it doubtless would have demolished us."

By the time they reached Idaho, one person "had accidentally shot and killed himself ... another had left us at Fort Laramie ... Three [others] turned back ... to return home."

Half of the party continued on to Oregon and the other half to California. "The days were very hot, the nights almost freezing. The first day our little company went only about ten miles ..."

They encountered "thickets so dense as to exclude the sun, and roaring little streams in deep, dark chasms ... paths which looked untrodden except by grizzly bears."

Name: _____ Date: _____

# Journal of a Pioneer (cont.)

## Extension

**Directions:** You are a pioneer child heading west. It's early morning on a hot, windy day. The temperature is already over 90 degrees. The wind blows the dust constantly across the prairie, getting inside everything. You're sweaty and dirty. You are thirsty, but the water barrel is almost empty. Write a journal entry about your experience. Describe your day in as much detail as possible.

# The Donner Tragedy

Everyone who traveled west by wagon train faced many **hardships** and difficulties. Considering the weather, mountains, deserts, lack of water, little food, hostile natives, sickness, and disease, it's a wonder so many actually completed the journey.

One of the most tragic stories was of a group of 87 men, women, and children who left Illinois in a wagon train headed for California in April 1846. For a time, they traveled with a much larger group. They then learned of an untried route recommended in *The Emigrant's Guide to Oregon and California,* which claimed the route would cut 300 miles from the journey. So the group, which was led by George Donner, split off from the larger party to try the new route.

Rather than being a shortcut, the route they chose caused many delays as they hacked a trail through the Wasatch Mountains in Utah and faced an 80-mile stretch of desert. They were **harassed** by hostile natives who stole their oxen. Arguments among members of the party led to several killings. Some wagons had to be abandoned along the way.

By the time they reached the Sierra Nevada Mountains, it was late in the season. Their supplies were running low. An intense, early **blizzard** forced them to turn back from the attempted crossing.

Some members of the party took shelter in an abandoned cabin, some built crude cabins, and others lived in tents while blizzards raged, day after day. In spite of several attempts to cross the mountains, only one group succeeded, and only seven of the 15 survived to reach Sutter's Fort, a distance of over 100 miles away. Rescuers tried many times to return for the rest of the group, but were unsuccessful because of the weather.

When rescue parties finally arrived four months later, those who were still alive were sick and starving. In desperation, some had resorted to cannibalism to survive. Of the original party, only 47 lived to see California.

One survivor, Virginia Reed, later wrote about the terrible winter they had spent waiting for rescue. "The **misery** endured during those four months at Donner Lake would fill pages and make the coldest heart ache."

In 1911, the book *The Expedition of the Donner Party and Its Tragic Fate*, written by Eliza Poor Donner Houghton, the youngest daughter of George and Tamsen Donner, was published. In the book, Eliza writes, ". . . I have always believed, that no one was to blame for the misfortunes which overtook us in the mountains. The dangers and difficulties encountered by reason of taking the Hastings Cut-off had all been **surmounted**—two weeks more and we should have reached our destination in safety. Then came the snow! Who could foresee that it would come earlier, fall deeper, and linger longer, that season than for thirty years before? Everything that a party could do to save itself was done by the Donner party..."

Name: _____  Date: _____

# The Donner Tragedy (cont.)

**Directions:** Complete the following activities.

## Matching

_____ 1. hardships

_____ 2. harassed

_____ 3. blizzard

_____ 4. misery

_____ 5. surmounted

a. severe snow storm

b. misfortune or difficulty

c. extreme unhappiness

d. to have overcome

e. to be annoyed or tormented

## Fill in the Blanks

1. The Donner party learned of an untried route recommended in *The Emigrant's Guide to Oregon and California,* which claimed the route would cut _____ miles from the journey.

2. By the time they reached the _____ _____ Mountains, it was late in the season.

3. In spite of several attempts to cross the mountains, only one group succeeded, and only seven of the 15 survived to reach _____ _____.

4. Of the original Donner party, only _____ lived to see California.

5. In 1911, the book *The Expedition of the Donner Party and Its Tragic Fate*, written by Eliza Poor Donner Houghton, the _____ daughter of George and Tamsen Donner, was published.

## Critical Thinking

If you had been with this group, would you have wanted to take an unknown "shortcut" or stay on the known routes? Give specific details and examples to support your answer.

_____

_____

_____

_____

_____

_____

_____

Name: _____ Date: _____

# Joseph Smith

Although the U.S. Constitution guarantees freedom of religion, members of the Church of Jesus Christ of Latter-day Saints, commonly called Mormons, were repeatedly denied that freedom.

The history of the Mormons began in New York. Joseph Smith, the founder of the group, said that an angel had told him where to find a book written on thin gold plates by the prophet Mormon. He translated the writings which became *The Book of Mormon*, the basis for the new religion.

As membership in the church grew, nonmembers became very hostile to Smith and his followers. The Mormons moved from western New York to Ohio, to Missouri, and then to Illinois in an attempt to be allowed to practice their religion in peace. Each time they established a settlement, they gained new converts; however, they also gained new enemies and were violently expelled by angry neighbors.

In Illinois, the Mormons founded the city of Nauvoo and began building a great temple. They also began practicing **polygamy**, having more than one wife, which Smith said was God's will.

**Joseph Smith**

Public outrage against polygamy was only one reason why Mormons were persecuted. People resented the Mormons' tendency to patronize only businesses owned by other Mormons. When Mormons voted, they all tended to vote for the same person. They also began a system of communal ownership of property that allowed church leaders to redistribute property to those in need.

When Smith announced he was running for president in 1844, he and his brother were arrested and murdered. His followers were threatened: if they stayed, they, too, would be killed.

**Graphic Organizer**

**Directions:** Complete the vocabulary chart by creating a definition, using the word in a sentence and drawing an illustration that helps you remember the meaning of the word.

| Word | Definition | Illustration |
|------|------------|--------------|
| **polygamy** | | |
| | Sentence | |

# Brigham Young

Brigham Young was born in Vermont. He was taken by his family to western New York, where a kind of religious **revival** was in progress. In 1829, the Youngs settled in Mendon, New York, some 40 miles from Palmyra and Fayette, where, a year later, Joseph Smith established the Church of Jesus Christ of Latter-day Saints.

When *The Book of Mormon* was given to him in 1830, Young studied it **assiduously** before eventually becoming a follower of Smith's new religion. He never looked back. He never had any doubts as to Smith's **divine** inspiration. His whole life was devoted to Mormonism.

In 1833, Young led his family and other converts to Kirtland, Ohio, where Mormons had begun to gather in 1830. Young eventually became a member of the Twelve Apostles, an administrative body that assisted Smith in directing the Church.

After Joseph Smith was killed, Brigham Young became the new Mormon leader. Young decided the Mormons would move to the area around the Great Salt Lake because there were no other settlers nearby. He began plans for the move by instructing people to grow extra crops, to store food, and to build wagons.

**Brigham Young**

In February 1846, the Mormons began leaving Nauvoo. By May, thousands were spread out across hundreds of miles of prairie. Those who went ahead set up camps and planted crops for those who followed. They spent the first winter near what is now Omaha, Nebraska. Many died that winter, but the survivors did not give up.

In the spring, Young led an advance party of 25 wagons to the valley of the Great Salt Lake. Two days after they arrived, men began planting crops to ensure there would be food for the others when they arrived. Young returned to join the main group and to lead them to their new home.

Besides being a strong religious leader, Brigham Young also had great **organizational** skills, which were **essential** in coordinating the move of thousands of people from Illinois to Utah. He also made arrangements for temporary quarters in Missouri for other converts from the United States and England who would later join them in Utah.

By 1870, the Mormon colonies had become examples of civic planning and foresight. Polygamy was still widespread, however, and it was not until 1890 that, on the promise of statehood for Utah, the Church changed its doctrine to ban polygamy. Brigham Young died in 1877.

UNIT TWO: WESTWARD EXPANSION & MIGRATION

# Brigham Young (cont.)

**Directions:** Complete the following activities.

## Matching

_____ 1. revival

_____ 2. assiduously

_____ 3. divine

_____ 4. organizational

_____ 5. essential

a. having the nature of God

b. necessary

c. with care and diligence

d. period of increased religious zeal

e. functional arrangement

## Fill in the Blanks

1. Brigham Young was born in _____.

2. His whole life was devoted to _____.

3. Young eventually became a member of the _____ _____, an administrative body that assisted Joseph Smith in directing the church.

4. After _____ _____ was killed, Brigham Young became the new Mormon leader.

5. In the spring of 1847, Young led an advance party of 25 wagons to the valley of the _____ _____ Lake.

## Constructed Response

What are at least three problems that Brigham Young had to deal with when thousands of Mormons left Illinois to travel west? Give specific details or examples to support your answer.

_____

_____

_____

_____

_____

_____

_____

_____

_____

_____

Name: _____  Date: _____

# The End of the Trail

After nearly six months of traveling, most wagon trains reached their destinations. Even those who had not met disasters along the way must have been worn out from the trip. But the hard work did not end when the journey was over. When people arrived at the end of the trail, their work was only beginning. They needed to claim land, build homes, plant fields, or open businesses.

For people arriving in Oregon, the first task was to file a claim for free land in Oregon City. Congress passed a bill in 1841 allowing each male settler to claim 640 acres of land; an additional 160 acres could be claimed for a wife and each child. Most people who traveled to Oregon settled in the Willamette River Valley, where trees were plentiful and winters were much milder than they had been in the East. This allowed them to plant winter wheat.

Many of the first homes people built were one-room log cabins. With help from neighbors, a log cabin could be erected fairly quickly. In the Southwest, wood was too scarce to use for building homes. Instead, people built with adobe. Adobe homes stay cool during hot days and retain warmth at night.

People ate, slept, cooked, and lived in homes that were quite small by today's standards. After living in a covered wagon for several months, however, any home, even a small one, must have seemed like a luxury.

## Graphic Organizer

**Directions:** Learn more abut the Preemption Act of 1841 and the Homestead Act of 1862. Using the T-chart below, compare the settlement rights of the two laws.

| Preemption Act of 1841 | Homestead Act of 1862 |
|---|---|
|  |  |

UNIT TWO: WESTWARD EXPANSION & MIGRATION

Name: _____ Date: _____

# Traveling by Sea

Not everyone who traveled to California and Oregon went overland. Some chose to make the trip by ship.

People living on or near the east coast could book passage on a clipper ship headed for California. The trip around Cape Horn was long, dangerous, and very expensive. Strong currents, icebergs, and fierce winds off Cape Horn caused ships to go off course, adding more time to the journey. The supply of ships did not nearly meet the demand for travel, and many older ships, which weren't very safe, were brought into service.

A second option was to sail across the Gulf of Mexico to Panama. From there, travelers walked or rode horses 100 miles through dense jungles to Panama City in the hopes of catching a ship heading north on the Pacific side. This route was also uncertain, long, and dangerous. Yellow fever, malaria, dysentery, and cholera killed many who attempted this route.

### Water Routes to California

| | |
|---|---|
| New York to Cape Horn | 15,000 miles—6–8 months |
| New York to Nicaragua | 5,500 miles—5 weeks |
| New York to Panama | 6,000 miles—6 weeks |
| New Orleans to Nicaragua | 4,500 miles—4 weeks |
| New Orleans to Panama | 5,000 miles—5 weeks |

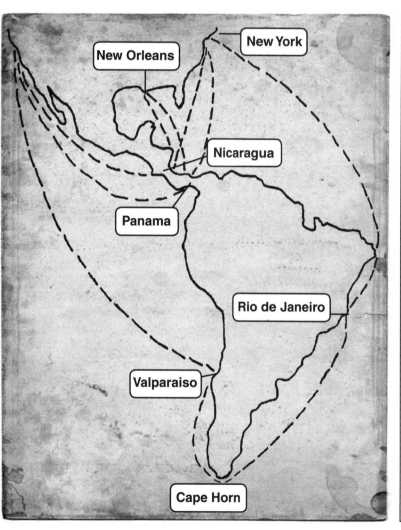

## Critical Thinking

Which method of travel would you have taken: overland in a covered wagon, by ship around Cape Horn, or by ship to Panama? Give specific details or examples to support your decision.

_____
_____
_____
_____
_____
_____
_____
_____
_____
_____
_____
_____

# Traveling By Stagecoach

Have you ever wondered what it would have been like to ride a stagecoach? Between 1850 and 1900, stagecoaches carried tens of thousands of passengers on regularly scheduled routes across the west. Compared to modern **transportation**, a stagecoach trip was painfully uncomfortable and dreadfully slow.

A newspaper printed this advice to passengers in 1877: "Don't imagine for a moment you are going on a picnic; expect annoyance, discomfort and some hardships. If you are disappointed, thank heaven."

Passengers traveling long distances carried weapons, blankets, water, and food with them. They rode day and night, averaging five to ten miles an hour. Most passengers rode on wooden benches inside the stagecoach. Mail, baggage, and sometimes passengers rode on seats outside or on the roof.

Stagecoaches were not heated or cooled. A blind covered the window, but didn't completely block snow, rain, wind, and dust. Coaches designed to hold nine passengers might actually carry 15 to 20 people. As coaches climbed hills or made turns, the passengers could be thrown from one side of the coach to the other. One reporter wrote: "The jolting will be found disagreeable at first, but a few nights without sleep **obviate** that difficulty."

In his book *Roughing It*, Mark Twain described his stagecoach experience:

*"Our coach was a great swinging and swaying stage, of the most sumptuous description—an imposing cradle on wheels...We began to get into country, now, threaded here and there with little streams. These had high, steep banks on each side, and every time we flew down one bank and scrambled up the other, our party got mixed somewhat. First we*

*would all be down in a pile at the forward end of the stage, nearly in a sitting posture, and in a second we would shoot to the other end, and stand on our heads. And we would sprawl and kick, too, and ward off ends and corners of mailbags that came lumbering over us and about us; and as the dust rose from the tumult, we would all sneeze in chorus, and the majority of us would grumble, and probably say some hasty thing, like: 'Take your elbow out of my ribs!—can't you quit crowding?'"*

Overloaded stagecoaches had a tendency to overturn. When the stagecoach came to a steep hill, mud, or soft sand, passengers had to get out and walk to lighten the load. Passengers faced other dangers, including runaway horses, bison stampedes, and attacks by robbers.

Relay stations every 10 to 25 miles provided rest stops. One passenger reported that at stagecoach stops "the available food would **curdle** a goat's stomach." Passengers also complained about the lack of **toilet** and bathing facilities at the rest stops. The trip from Missouri to California took about a month.

Name: _____  Date: _____

# Traveling by Stagecoach (cont.)

**Directions:** Complete the following activities.

## Matching

_____ 1. transportation

_____ 2. obviate

_____ 3. sumptuous

_____ 4. curdle

_____ 5. toilet

a. make unnecessary

b. bathroom

c. magnificent or splendid

d. to turn sour

e. method of moving goods and people from one place to another

## Fill in the Blanks

1. Passengers traveling long distances carried _____, _____, _____, and food with them.

2. A blind covered the _____, but it didn't completely block snow, rain, wind, and dust.

3. Coaches designed to hold _____ passengers might actually carry from 15 to 20 people.

4. Overloaded stagecoaches had a tendency to _____.

5. The trip from Missouri to California took about a _____.

## Critical Thinking

Which method of transportation would you have preferred, wagon train or stagecoach? Give specific details or examples to support your answer.

_____

_____

_____

_____

_____

_____

_____

_____

_____

_____

# The Pony Express

As more people moved west, the need for quicker **communication** became more pressing. News could be carried by ship or stagecoach from the east coast to California, but even the fastest methods took nearly a month—much too long for businessmen.

The **solution**: use the existing stagecoach stops and add more to establish a system of stations every 10 to 20 miles where riders could change horses quickly. Every 75 to 100 miles, fresh riders took over for exhausted ones. By traveling day and night, riders covered the 2,000-mile trip between St. Joseph, Missouri, and Sacramento, California, in ten days.

The first ad for Pony Express riders was placed in March 1860. A month later, the first rider left St. Joseph, Missouri.

**WANTED**

Young, skinny, wiry fellows not over 20. Must be expert riders willing to risk death daily. Orphans preferred. Wages: $25 a week.

This ad was answered by many young men, including Bill Cody, age 14. The youngest rider, Bronco Charlie Miller, began his career at the age of 11 when a riderless horse with a mail **pouch** arrived in Sacramento. He took the mail on to the next station, was hired, and continued as a Pony Express rider for five months.

Eventually, the Pony Express had over 100 stations, 80 riders, and 400 to 500 horses. Although the route was extremely dangerous, only one mail delivery was lost during the time the Pony Express was in operation.

Pony Express riders brought news of Abraham Lincoln's election in 1860 and the beginning of the Civil War in 1861 to California. **Financially**, it was a failure, even though it cost $5 to send mail by Pony Express. The Pony Express closed in October 1861 when the Pacific Telegraph Company completed a line to San Francisco. During its 19 months of **operation**, Pony Express riders covered 650,000 miles and carried 34,753 pieces of mail.

**Think About It**

The youngest Pony Express rider, Bronco Charlie Miller, lived to the age of 105. When the Korean War began, he tried to enlist but was turned down. He was 92 years old at the time.

UNIT TWO: WESTWARD EXPANSION & MIGRATION

Name: _____  Date: _____

# The Pony Express (cont.)

**Directions:** Complete the following activities.

## Matching

_____  1.  communication

_____  2.  solution

_____  3.  pouch

_____  4.  financially

_____  5.  operation

a.  refers to money

b.  transferring of information

c.  process of functioning

d.  resolution of a problem

e.  bag

## Fill in the Blanks

1.  News could be carried by _____ or _____ from the east coast to California, but even the fastest methods took nearly a month—much too long for businessmen.

2.  Every 75 to _____ miles, fresh riders took over for exhausted ones.

3.  The first ad for Pony Express riders was placed in March _____.

4.  Eventually, the Pony Express had over 100 _____, 80 _____, and 400 to 500 horses.

5.  It cost $_____ to send mail by Pony Express.

## Critical Thinking

What other qualities or skills besides those listed in the ad do you think a Pony Express rider needed? Give specific details or examples to support your opinion.

_____

_____

_____

_____

_____

_____

_____

_____

_____

_____

_____

# The Transcontinental Telegraph

The telegraph, invented by Samuel Morse, used electricity to send messages over wires strung on poles. He sent his first long-distance message in 1844 from Washington, D.C., to Baltimore, Maryland.

**Samuel Morse**

Telegraph operators sent messages using a system called Morse code. Each letter of the alphabet was represented by a different combination of dots (short pulses) and dashes (longer pulses). The person who received the messages translated the code and wrote out the letters and words.

By 1860, most cities on the east coast were connected by telegraph. Slowly the lines were extended westward.

The Western Union Telegraph Company received a government contract to connect telegraph lines from Missouri to Salt Lake City, where another line was already connected to San Francisco.

Thousands of wooden poles were needed to carry the wires across a 1,000-mile area with few trees. About 100 freight wagons carried the poles, the wire, the workers, and the supplies needed to dig the holes, erect the poles, and string the wires.

Once the project was finally completed, keeping the telegraph working became a full-time job for a large crew of workers called linemen. Sometimes wires were deliberately cut. Wind and heavy snow could snap wires. Lightning frequently hit the wires.

One menace to the telegraph lines came from an unexpected source. Bison discovered that telegraph poles were great back scratchers! As the great shaggy animals took turns rubbing against the poles, their heavy sideways movements knocked the poles over. Adding long metal spikes to discourage them only provided more efficient back scratchers.

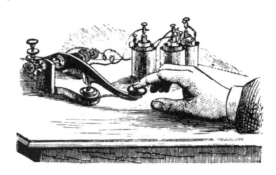

**UNIT TWO: WESTWARD EXPANSION & MIGRATION**

## Activity

**Directions:** People who sent telegrams paid by the word, so they used as few words as possible. On the lines below, rewrite this message in nine words or less.

Dear Mom and Dad, Your first grandchild, a healthy baby boy, was born yesterday at 5 P.M. We named him Adam Jesse James Winthrop. He has red hair just like Grandpa Joe and eyes like Grandma Eleanor. Alice is tired, but well. Love, your son, Jim.

_____

_____

# Morse Code

| A | •— | H | •••• | O | ——— | U | ••— |
|---|----|---|------|---|------|---|-----|
| B | —••• | I | •• | P | •——• | V | •••— |
| C | —•—• | J | •——— | Q | ——•— | W | •—— |
| D | —•• | K | —•— | R | •—• | X | —••— |
| E | • | L | •—•• | S | ••• | Y | —•—— |
| F | ••—• | M | —— | T | — | Z | ——•• |
| G | ——• | N | —• |   |   |   |   |

1. Use Morse code to decipher this message.

— •••• •    — • •—•• • ——• •—• •—••—• ••••    •—— •— •••

—    —— —    ——    —    ——    —    —    ——    —    —

•— ——• •—• • •— —    ••—• •—• ••• — • —• — • •• ——— —•

——    —    ——    —    ——    —    —    ——    —    —

2. Write your own message in Morse code and have a partner translate it. Use the code for one letter above each blank. Skip a blank between words.

___ ___ ___ ___ ___ ___ ___ ___ ___ ___ ___ ___ ___ ___ ___ ___

___ ___ ___ ___ ___ ___ ___ ___ ___ ___ ___ ___ ___ ___ ___ ___

___ ___ ___ ___ ___ ___ ___ ___ ___ ___ ___ ___ ___ ___ ___ ___

___ ___ ___ ___ ___ ___ ___ ___ ___ ___ ___ ___ ___ ___ ___ ___

___ ___ ___ ___ ___ ___ ___ ___ ___ ___ ___ ___ ___ ___ ___ ___

Name: _____   Date: _____

# The Transcontinental Railroad

During the 1840s and 1850s, railroads had become a major means of transportation along the east coast. People and goods could travel more quickly and comfortably by railroad than by any other means available.

The dream of a railroad stretching from one coast to the other became a possibility when the Pacific Railway Bill was passed in 1862; however, the project was delayed until 1865 because of the Civil War.

The Union Pacific Railroad began laying track in Omaha, Nebraska, heading west. At the same time, the Central Pacific Railroad started laying track in Sacramento, California, heading east. To complete the project, the federal government granted the two railroads loans of nearly $65 million and ownership of approximately 24 million acres of land.

The project involved laying about 1,700 miles of track across prairies, deserts, mountains, and valleys. Most of the workers were **immigrants**. The Central Pacific imported 10,000 Chinese laborers. The Union Pacific hired mostly Irish immigrants.

Building the transcontinental railroad was not an easy task. Workers needed food, supplies, and shelter. Working conditions were dangerous. The weather caused problems and delays. Native Americans resented the encroachment of the "**iron horse**" on their lands and tried to prevent the railroad from being completed.

On May 10, 1869, the two railroads met at Promontory Point, Utah, where representatives of both railroads drove a golden spike into the final rails. Once the railroad was completed, it was possible to travel from coast to coast in a week!

### Technology in the Classroom

**Primary Source:** <http://hdl.loc.gov/loc.rbc/rbpe.08600600>
("Go west over the Missouri Pacific or Atlantic & Pacific railroad, via Saint Louis [Time tables, rates, etc.] St. Louis [186-?]," Library of Congress American Memory)

**Directions:** The transcontinental railroad connected the United States from East to West, allowing the nation to become a mobile society. Examine the primary source. Image you are traveling west on the train. Integrating information taken from the documents, design individual railroad tickets for a family of four (two adults, one 10-year-old child, and one 3-year-old child) from St. Louis to a destination of your choice in the West. Be sure to include information such as starting and ending destination points, price of the ticket, class (example: first class), rules, etc.

UNIT TWO: WESTWARD EXPANSION & MIGRATION

# Homes of the Settlers

On the plains where there were few trees, earth was the only material available for building, so that's what the settlers used. Bricks of sod about one foot wide, two feet long, and four inches thick were cut from the prairie. Each brick weighed about 50 pounds; cutting enough bricks of sod was backbreaking work. The long, tough roots of prairie grasses were difficult to **hack** through. The cut bricks were then stacked, grass side down, to build the walls for one-room houses. Boards were laid over the doors and windows to support more bricks. For the roof, the settlers used a frame of poles covered with brush and more sod. The floor was packed-down dirt.

Nicknamed "soddies," these homes provided **insulation** against heat and cold. They didn't burn easily, like wooden homes. However, the homes were damp and musty most of the time, and they were impossible to keep clean all of the time.

Bits of dirt frequently dropped from the ceiling and walls when it was dry. When it rained, the floor and walls turned to mud. Mice, bugs, and snakes felt more at home in the sod houses than the settlers did, and the settlers weren't too happy about having to share their homes.

Settlers on the prairies had to contend with extreme heat, bitter cold, droughts, floods, wind, and snow. Lack of trees meant lack of firewood for cooking and heat; instead, dried bison dung was burned. Water was also in short supply and often had to be carried long distances. In summer, even wells and streams could dry up.

Another big problem with life on the prairie was the **isolation**. The nearest neighbor might be 10, 20, or more miles away.

One reason people stayed, even under such harsh conditions, was because the Homestead Act of 1862 allowed the head of a household to pay a small filing fee for 160 acres of land. If the family lived on the land and farmed it for five years, it was theirs free.

In Oregon where wood was plentiful, people built log cabins or wooden frame houses. If people lived near a sawmill, they could buy wooden planks to build a frame house. If not, they usually built log cabins.

To build log cabins, people cut down trees, stripped off the bark, and cut the logs to the same length. Then the logs were **notched** on the ends so they would fit together as they were laid one on top of the other to build the walls.

Small windows and a door were cut out of the log walls. Windows were covered with glass, **parchment**, animals skins, or wooden shutters. Doors were made of wood or animal hides. The final step was to build a roof of wooden shingles and fill in the spaces between the logs with wood chips, moss, mud, or clay.

Name: _____    Date: _____

# Homes of the Settlers (cont.)

**Directions:** Complete the following activities.

## Matching

_____ 1. hack

_____ 2. insulation

_____ 3. isolation

_____ 4. notched

_____ 5. parchment

a. the state of separation from others

b. material that protects from heat or cold

c. thin material made from an animal skin

d. cut

e. cut an indentation into wood

## Fill in the Blanks

1. On the plains where there were few trees, _____ was the only material available for building, so that's what the settlers used.

2. Settlers on the prairies had to contend with extreme _____, bitter cold, _____, floods, wind, and snow.

3. The Homestead Act of 1862 allowed the head of a household to pay a small filing fee for _____ acres of land.

4. If settlers in Oregon lived near a _____, they could buy wooden planks to build a frame house.

5. The logs were notched on the ends so they would fit _____ as they were laid one on top of the other to build the walls.

## Critical Thinking

Would you rather live in a log cabin or a soddy? Give specific details or examples to support your opinion.

_____

_____

_____

_____

_____

_____

_____

_____

UNIT TWO: WESTWARD EXPANSION & MIGRATION

# Major John Wesley Powell

**John Wesley Powell**

John Wesley Powell was born in Mount Morris, New York, on March 24, 1834. His family moved to Ohio, and in 1846, they moved to a farm in Wisconsin. It was at this farm where John developed his life-long interest in the study of Native Americans and **ethnology**. He attended college in Illinois.

In 1861, John Powell enlisted in the Union Army. By 1863, he had risen to the rank of Major. He lost an arm in the Battle of Shiloh. In 1865, he resigned from the army. After two years as a professor of geology, he began his famous exploration of the Colorado River.

On May 24, 1869, Major John Powell and a crew of nine began a journey to explore the length of the Colorado River. They loaded enough supplies for ten months on their four boats and set off from Green River Station in Wyoming and down the Green River.

The men reached the first canyon three days later and named it "Flaming Gorge," for its **brilliant** orange and red rocks. Here they found fossils of ancient **marine** animals that had lived in the oceans that had once covered the western part of North America.

When they reached steep waterfalls or rapids, the men tied ropes to the boats and stood on the shore on both sides of the river to lower them over the waterfalls. Then they carried their supplies down steep, rocky trails to the bottom. At some points, they even had to carry their boats.

Early in June, a boat carrying three men went over a waterfall. The men were saved, but about 2,000 pounds of supplies were lost. A fire at their campsite on June 16 destroyed more of their supplies. At times, the men became discouraged because of the hard work, mosquitoes, and heat.

After almost two months of travel covering 538 miles, the group reached the Colorado River. Although one member left the group, the others continued their journey through beautiful canyons and around **cataracts**, rapids, and waterfalls. On August 10, they reached the Grand Canyon. By then, their clothes and shoes were falling apart, and they had only a month's worth of supplies left. They also knew that more dangers lay ahead.

When they came to the most dangerous rapids they had encountered so far, three of the men decided not to continue and headed back on foot.

With only two boats and no supplies, the remaining six men finally reached a Mormon **settlement** on the Virgin River. There they ended their 100-day adventure.

**The Grand Canyon**

Name: _____ Date: _____

# Major John Wesley Powell (cont.)

**Directions:** Complete the following activities.

## Matching

_____ 1. ethnology

_____ 2. brilliant

_____ 3. marine

_____ 4. cataracts

_____ 5. settlement

a. community of people, but smaller than a town

b. division of anthropology dealing with comparing cultures

c. bright

d. pertaining to the sea

e. large waterfalls

## Fill in the Blanks

1. John Wesley Powell was born in Mount Morris, _____ _____ on March 24, 1834.

2. In 1861, John Powell enlisted in the _____ Army.

3. When they reached steep waterfalls or rapids, the men tied _____ to the boats and stood on the shore on both sides of the river to lower them over the waterfalls.

4. After almost _____ months of travel covering _____ miles, the group reached the Colorado River.

5. With only two boats and no supplies, the remaining six men finally reached a _____ settlement on the Virgin River.

## Critical Thinking

John Wesley Powell became Commissioner of Indian Affairs in 1873. Learn more about Major Powell and list five of his achievements below.

_____

_____

_____

_____

_____

_____

_____

UNIT TWO: WESTWARD EXPANSION & MIGRATION

Name: _____ Date: _____

# Word Search: What Did They Take?

**Directions:** Look up, down, backward, forward, and diagonally to find and circle in the puzzle the 50 words listed below. These are all items that pioneers might have taken on the Santa Fe and Oregon Trails.

```
Q N N X W F J M S Z N R V K K K R N W S N E P X
P R C T T X T M R L B R E Y C P Z A A M Y J G G
R L S O A P Y V O A J K L P X N D T S R T K H N
M K D A E L W N S N L N C R P O N S H A L K M P
V T H T J P X G S T K L B L S E E Y T Z H K S W
L R J G A X N N I E L M N G R S P R U O N W K J
C Y Z P C I B N C R Z H N R S K R N B R O C R Q
O B E R H O T R S N G I L A Q B E A N S C P O H
W R T T W R J U L W K C L T Q L M G F H A A F T
G V O L B R M H T A V O T K E T T L E S B N N E
G L S F O K E C B L M N Q R G N T B Q Z K N L N
C V L L O W P T V M A M E U B P M U L E P O T I
N R K T K H K H A C B S Q E I E N K X G M K L C
V N L Y S V R N N W N D R B D L D R C I Q T N I
T I U R F D E I R D W J N Q J L T D H P E X J D
K C S C O F F E E C H S M C L Z E F I N G W C E
R T Z E J E M V G M D B R Q F A L S T N O F K M
W U S L H J L M H E K A M J Q W D K J L G N L P
L L O U K C K D E T C H S U R B R L P L I Q G R
T V F L G R T S N K M L W R K H T T E S L O O T
G M B Z F A Q A E A P C E L F I R E H R P T L R
P V R K H T R R M V C G O B G N K A I X R A P N
V P W N R N S W L K P C L M G X P C Q L R Y Q N
J F W H E T S T O N E F K W B W E F R D F Q G K
```

| | | | | |
|---|---|---|---|---|
| BACON | COFFEE | LANTERN | PENS | SCISSORS |
| BAKING SODA | COMB | LARD | PEPPER | SEEDS |
| BEANS | COW | LEAD | PIG | SOAP |
| BEDDING | CRACKERS | MATCHES | PLOW | SUGAR |
| BOOKS | DRIED FRUIT | MEDICINE | POT | TEA |
| BOWLS | FLOUR | MOLASSES | QUILT | TENT |
| BRUSH | FORKS | MULE | RAZOR | TOOLS |
| CANDLE | INK | NEEDLES | RICE | WASHTUB |
| CHURN | KETTLES | PAN | RIFLE | WATER |
| CLOTHING | LADLE | PAPER | SALT | WHETSTONE |

Name: _____    Date: _____

# Western Heroes and Heroines

## Research

**Directions:** Learn more about the life of one of the people listed below. Using the information, design a trading card. On the front side of the trading card, place the name of your person and a picture. If a picture is not available, use a picture that would symbolize the person's life. On the back side of the card, list interesting facts about the person's life and experiences in the West. Use the template at the bottom of the page as an example.

| | | |
|---|---|---|
| John Ashley | John Colter | James Marshall |
| Moses Austin | Davy Crockett | Joe Meek |
| Edward Beale | Mike Fink | Annie Oakley |
| William Becknell | Thomas Fitzpatrick | Zebulon Pike |
| Charles Bent | John C. Frémont | George Sibley |
| John Bidwell | Josiah Gregg | Jedediah Smith |
| Daniel Boone | Wild Bill Hickok | Eliza Spaulding |
| Jim Bridger | Sam Houston | Henry Spaulding |
| Kit Carson | Henrietta Chamberlain King | General Zachary Taylor |
| George Catlin | Baptiste La Lande | Louis Vasquez |
| William Clark | Meriwether Lewis | Marcus Whitman |
| Buffalo Bill Cody | Major Stephen Long | Narcissa Whitman |
| Samuel Colt | Susan Magoffin | Brigham Young |

Front of Card

Back of Card

**NAME OF PERSON**

Insert
Picture or Illustration

**INTERESTING FACTS**

- Fact One
- Fact Two
- Fact Three
- Fact Four
- Fact Five
- Fact Six

*Western Heroes and Heroines Trading Card Series*

Name: _____ Date: _____

# Native Americans in the West

Hundreds of groups of Native Americans lived in U.S. territories west of the Mississippi River from the Canadian border to Mexico and west to the Pacific coast. Many had very distinctive lifestyles and cultures. Eventual domination by white society was the only thing they all had in common.

## NATIVE AMERICAN TRIBAL REGIONS

**PLAINS**
Blackfoot
Gros Ventre
Hidatsa
Crow
Mandan
Yanktonai Sioux
Aikara
Shoshone
Cheyenne
Teton Sioux
Ponca
Yankton Sioux
Omaha
Pawnee
Oto
Arapaho
Kansa
Missouri
Kiowa
Osage
Quapaw
Comanche
Wichita
Kichai
Tawakoni
Tonkawa
Lipan Apache

**SOUTHWEST**
Havasupai
Huzlapai
Mojave
Halchidhoma
Yuma

Cocopa
Pima
Navajo
Zuni
Yavapai
Maricopa
Aravaipa Apache
Jicarilla Apache
Coyotera Apache
Hopi
Papago
Tiwa
Tewa
Towa
Keres
Mimbreno

**CALIFORNIA/
INTERMOUNTAIN**
Northern Paiute
Tolowa
Karok
Yurok
Shasta
Wiyot
Achomaui
Wintun
Hupa
Bannock
Northern Shoshone
Chimariko
Asatsagewi
Yana
Washoe
Nomlaki

Yahi
Western
  Shoshone
Yuki
Maidu
Pomo
Konkow
Gosiute
Ute
Paiute
Wappo
Miwok
Kawaiisu
Patwin
Mono
Panamint
Costano
Yokut
Chemehuevi
Esselen
Tubatulabal
Salina
Kitanemuk
Serrano
Chumash
Fernandeno
Gabrielino
Juaneno
Cahuilla
Luiseno
Cupeno
Diegueno
Kamia
Akwa'ala
Nakipa

Kiliwa
Cochimi
Ignacieno
Waicura
Pericu

**PLATEAU**
Sanpoil
Chelan
Columbia
Kootenay
Coleville
Pend d'Oreille
Coeur d'Alene
Flathead
Nez Percé
Cayuse
Spokane
Walla Walla
Umatilla
Klickitat
Yakama
Wishram
Tenino
Molala
Wanapam
Klamath
Modoc

**PACIFIC
NORTHWEST**
Skagit
Quileute
Quinault
Humptulips
Chehalis
Skokomish
Chimakurn
Duwamish
Snogualmie
Puyallup
Coast Salis
Chinook
Clatsop
Clatskanie
Tillamook
Siletz
Yaquina
Siuslaw
Coos
Umpqua
Tututni
Chastacosta
Makah
Coulitz

UNIT TWO: WESTWARD EXPANSION & MIGRATION

Name: _____ Date: _____

# Native Americans in the West (cont.)

**Directions:** In the center of the circle, write the name of a Native American tribe. Research the tribe to find information on the tribe's food, clothing, arts and crafts, housing, location, and government/religion. Write the information you find in the appropriate section of the circle.

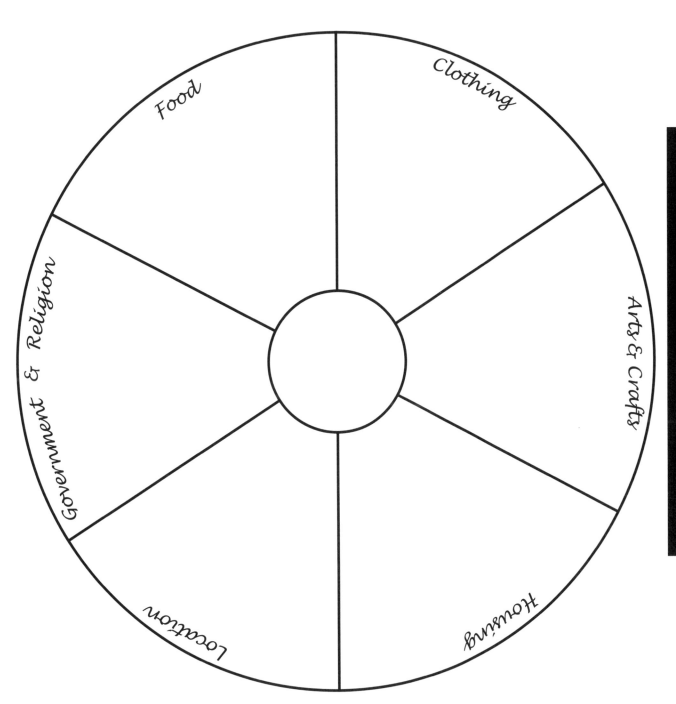

# Time Line of the Gold Rush

1834       John Sutter emigrated to the United States.

1842       Don Francisco Lopez discovered gold in the roots of an onion at Placeritas Canyon in the San Fernando Valley.

1846 –     The Mexican War was fought between the United States and Mexico.
  1848

1847       Yerba Buena was renamed the Town of San Francisco.

1848       **January:** James Marshall discovered gold while building a lumber mill for John Sutter.

**February:** The United States gained Arizona, California, Nevada, New Mexico, Utah, and western Colorado from Mexico after the Mexican War.

**March:** The *California Star* reported the non-native population of San Francisco was 575 males, 177 females, and 60 children.

**March:** Gold was discovered by Mormons on the south fork of the American River.

**March:** The *Californian* printed the first story of the gold discovery.

**July 18:** Word of the gold strike reached Los Angeles.

**September:** Gold dust was worth $16 an ounce.

**November:** Zachary Taylor was elected president.

1849       **February:** The first ship carrying prospectors arrived in California.

**April:** Wagon trains with 20,000 people were headed for the Gold Rush.

**December:** By the end of this year, 80,000 had arrived in California in search of gold. Army records show that 716 enlisted men deserted between July 1, 1848, and December 31, 1849.

**December:** The population of San Francisco was estimated at 15,000.

1850       **July:** President Taylor died; Millard Fillmore became president.

**September:** California became a state.

Name: _____   Date: _____

# Gold Rush Time Line Activity

**Directions:** Number the events in order from 1 (first) to 10 (last). Use the time line for reference.

_____ A.   The first ship carrying prospectors arrived in California.

_____ B.   The population of San Francisco was estimated at 15,000.

_____ C.   Franklin Pierce was elected president of the United States.

_____ D.   The *Californian* printed the first story of the gold discovery.

_____ E.   John Sutter emigrated to the United States.

_____ F.   Wagon trains with 20,000 people were headed for the Gold Rush.

_____ G.   California joined the Union as a state.

_____ H.   President Taylor died and Millard Fillmore became president.

_____ I.   Yerba Buena was renamed the Town of San Francisco.

_____ J.   James Marshall discovered gold at Sutter's mill.

---

## Graphic Organizer

**Directions:** Choose 10 events from the time line. Create an illustrated time line featuring these events. Cut a piece of yarn two yards long. On a plain 3″ x 5″ index card, place the name and date of the event, draw a picture of the event, and write one sentence describing it. Punch a hole in the top of the card and tie it to your yarn time line in the appropriate place. Repeat this procedure with the other events. Be sure to put the cards in chronological order and leave enough string on both ends to allow you to display your time line.

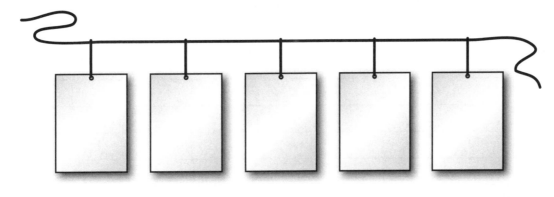

83

Name: _____  Date: _____

# Gold Fever

Gold Fever infected tens of thousands of people in North and South America, Europe, and Asia. It affected people of every age, social class, and occupation—farmers, merchants, doctors, lawyers, rich men, and poor ones. Everyone with gold fever had one common goal—to cure the fever by searching for gold in California.

**Think About It**
Why do you think people called it "gold fever"?

The fever began with the discovery of gold by James Marshall in January 1848 at the site where a mill was being built on land owned by John Sutter. He reportedly stated, "Hey boys, … I believe I've found a gold mine!"

As soon as this news spread, people swarmed to northern California using every means of transportation available. Fortune seekers walked, rode horses or mules, traveled in wagons and stagecoaches, or sailed thousands of miles in search of a dream.

What happened to John Sutter and James Marshall, the one who owned the land and the one who found the gold that began the mad rush to California? Did they cure the fever? Did thousands of miners become rich beyond their wildest dreams?

For most, that dream turned into a nightmare of hardship, disease, poverty, and sometimes death. For every prospector who found enough gold to become wealthy, thousands more lost everything they had and left the gold fields poorer than when they arrived.

Most who traveled to California in search of gold never intended to stay. They planned to make their fortunes, return home, and continue with their normal lives, but it rarely happened that way. Whether they found gold or not, stayed or returned home, everyone who traveled to California found that life was never the same again.

## Critical Thinking

How was gold fever like a disease? Give specific details or examples to support your answer.

_____

_____

_____

_____

_____

_____

UNIT THREE: GOLD RUSH

Name: _____ Date: _____

# What Is Gold?

Gold is a rare soft metal found in nature. Only five-billionths of Earth's crust is gold.

Gold has been prized for thousands of years. Because it is soft, it is easier to work with than other metals. When heated to 1,943°F, gold melts and becomes liquid. Melted gold can be poured into various shapes. Gold can be hammered into sheets thinner than most paper or made into a fine thread.

In nature, gold is usually found mixed with other minerals. A combination of minerals that includes some gold is called gold ore. Small flakes of gold are easier to find than gold **nuggets**. Most nuggets are small, but one found in Australia weighed 152 pounds!

Gold is 19.3 times denser than water. Pure gold is 24 karats, but it is too soft for most uses. When gold is mixed with other

metals, it becomes harder and stronger than pure gold. Most gold used for jewelry is an alloy, or mixed with silver or other metals. To keep it safe, gold is formed into bullion, or bars, and kept in bank vaults.

## Research

**Directions:** Learn more about the element gold. Use the information to fill in the blanks below.

1. Atomic Number       _____        2. Symbol                     _____
3. Family Name         _____        4. Solid, Liquid or Gas      _____
5. Metal, Nonmetal,    _____        6. Natural or Manmade        _____
   or Metalloid                             7. Radioactive or Stable     _____

## Graphic Organizer

**Directions:** Complete the vocabulary chart by creating a definition, using the word in a sentence and drawing an illustration that helps you remember the meaning of the word.

| Word | Definition | Illustration |
|------|------------|--------------|
| **nugget** | | |
| | Sentence | |

Name: _____  Date: _____

# Gold Discovered at Sutter's Mill

**James Marshall**

James Marshall, construction supervisor of a sawmill being built for John Sutter, was trying to solve problems that prevented the water from flowing forcefully enough to keep the waterwheel turning properly. He had workers deepening and widening the waterway. Each morning he checked the work and the flow of the water.

On the morning of January 24, 1848, Marshall was checking the progress of the work when he noticed a few glittering flakes of gold. Returning quickly to the mill, Marshall shouted to the men, "Hey, boys, ... I believe I have found a gold mine!"

In an interview some years later, Marshall described the day he discovered gold at Sutter's mill.

"One morning in January, it was a clear, cold morning; I shall never forget that morning. I was taking my usual walk along the race after shutting off the water, my eye was caught with the glimpse of something shining in the bottom of the ditch. There was about a foot of water running then. I reached my hand down and picked it up; it made my heart thump, for I was certain it was gold." ... James W. Marshall

After collecting more samples over the next few days, Marshall hurried to Sacramento to tell John Sutter the big news.

---

## Research

**Directions:** A **cause** is an event that produces a result. An **effect** is the result produced, or what happens. Learn more about the causes and effects of the California Gold Rush of 1849. For each cause below, write an effect.

1. Cause: James Marshall discovered gold.
   Effect: _____

2. Cause: Tens of thousands of miners traveled to California in 1849.
   Effect: _____

3. Cause: Prices in California were very high during the Gold Rush era.
   Effect: _____

4. Cause: Crime was high in mining camps.
   Effect: _____

# John Sutter

When **John Sutter** arrived in California in 1839, that area was still part of Mexico. He convinced the Mexican government to give him 50,000 acres of land in the Sacramento Valley. After the Mexican War ended in 1848, California became part of the United States.

Sutter built a fort of adobe bricks near where the American and Sacramento Rivers joined. In time, he owned thousands of cattle, horses, sheep, and pigs; he controlled ranches, a gristmill, a tannery, and a hat factory. He also had a bakery and blanket factory, as well as spinning, weaving, blacksmith, carpentry, and shoemaking businesses.

When **James Marshall** brought him proof of the discovery of gold, Sutter asked Marshall to keep his discovery a secret. Marshall agreed. The workers also promised to keep the discovery secret until the mill was finished.

A secret is difficult to keep, however, especially one as exciting as the discovery of gold. Even Sutter himself could not keep quiet. Within days of the discovery, he wrote in a letter: "I have made a discovery of a gold mine which, according to the experiments we have made, is extremely rich."

A few days after Sutter learned about the gold, Jacob Wittmer, a teamster employed by Sutter, received some gold when he delivered supplies to the mill. When he returned to the fort, he used the gold to buy brandy. Soon everyone at the fort knew.

Sutter's secret made it to San Francisco as early as March 15, 1848. The news appeared as a small notice on the last page of the *Californian*. However, this announcement didn't have much effect on the people of San Francisco.

John Sutter's road to California was a long one. In 1834, he left his home in Switzerland to escape his business debts and immigrated to America. He traveled to Fort Vancouver in the Oregon Territory, visited Alaska, and sailed to the Hawaiian Islands before settling in California.

THE CALIFORNIAN               MARCH 15, 1848

GOLD MINE FOUND:
In the newly made raceway of the Saw Mill recently erected by Captain Sutter, on the American Fork, gold has been found in considerable quantities. One person brought thirty dollars worth to New Helvetia, gathered there in a short time. California, no doubt, is rich in mineral wealth, great chances here for scientific capitalists. Gold has been found in almost every part of the country.

**Text of the article that appeared in the March 15, 1848, edition of the *Californian* newspaper.**

UNIT THREE: GOLD RUSH

Name: _____  Date: _____

# John Sutter (cont.)

In May 1848, Sam Brannan, a Mormon elder, visited Sutter's Mill. Excited about finding gold, he returned to San Francisco. Waving a bottle of gold dust, he shouted "Gold! Gold! Gold from the American River!" The news was like lighting a stick of dynamite; everyone exploded.

Gold fever struck immediately after Sam Brannan made his announcement. Within days, the city was nearly empty. The *Californian* suspended publication on May 29 with these words.

*"The majority of our subscribers and many of our advertisers have closed their doors and places of business and left town ... The whole country, from San Francisco to Los Angeles and from the seashore to the Sierra Nevada, resounds with the sordid cry of gold! Gold!! Gold, while the field is left half-planted, the house half-built, and everything neglected but the manufacture of shovels and pickaxes."*

## Matching

_____ 1. John Sutter

_____ 2. James Marshall

a. discovered gold at Sutter's Mill

b. gold discovered on his land started the California Gold Rush of 1849

## Multiple Choice

1. When John Sutter arrived in California in 1839, that area was still part of what country?
   - a. Spain
   - b. Mexico
   - c. Canada
   - d. Great Britain

2. Gold fever struck immediately after this man announced gold had been found in the American River.
   - a. John Sutter
   - b. James Marshall
   - c. Sam Brannan
   - d. President Polk

## Critical Thinking

Why do you think John Sutter wanted to keep the discovery of gold on his property a secret? Give specific details or examples to support your answer.

_____

_____

_____

_____

_____

_____

Name: _____ Date: _____

# Guidebooks to the Gold Rush

"Don't believe everything you read" is good advice today. It was even better advice during the Gold Rush.

*Three Weeks in the Gold Mines,* written by Henry Simpson, claimed his partner had found a gold nugget "about as large and thick as my double hands outspread." It was a good story, but completely untrue. The title implied that people could quickly find large chunks of gold. Books like Simpson's caused even those with a mild case of gold fever to become strongly infected, ready to risk everything and rush to California.

A variety of guidebooks were published during this time offering advice to people traveling to the gold fields. Many of the useless guidebooks were written by armchair experts who had never been west of the Mississippi River.

Some guidebooks were downright dangerous because of the amount of inaccurate or false information they contained. They included hearsay and rumors reported as truth, parts of government documents, newspaper clippings, and inaccurate maps. Some authors suggested the worst possible routes to take and underplayed the hardships of the journey. "The journey is one of the most delightful and invigorating," claimed one source.

However, some of the guidebooks were authentic. They offered good advice, helpful tips, practical suggestions, and a realistic description of the journey and hardships.

## Did You Know?

The first recorded discovery of gold in California occurred in 1842 when Don Francisco Lopez discovered the precious metal at Placeritas Canyon in the San Fernando Valley, about 40 miles northwest of Los Angeles. While digging onions, he noticed something glittering among the roots. Within a few weeks, hundreds of people went to the area to try their luck. The deposits were worked successfully for a number of years but were eventually depleted and forgotten.

**Technology in the Classroom**
**Primary Source:** <http://www.library.ca.gov/goldrush/images/emigrant_guide_cover.jpg>
("The Emigrant's Guide to the Gold Mines," State of California.)

**Directions:** Examine "The Emigrant's Guide to the Gold Mines," found at the primary source website above. Find out more about travel west to the gold fields. Design a prospector's guide to the gold mines. Offer the traveler good advice, helpful tips, practical suggestions, and a realistic description of the journey and hardships.

UNIT THREE: GOLD RUSH

# The Forty-Niners

News of gold found at Sutter's Mill and other places in California caused one of the largest and wildest migrations in history. Between 75,000 and 100,000 people made their way to the California gold fields in 1849. Nicknamed **forty-niners**, most of the gold seekers were men. By 1850, women accounted for only eight percent of the population of California.

The news of gold spread by ship to Hawaii and Oregon. By mid-summer, settlers in Oregon were pulling up stakes and heading south to join the Gold Rush.

In July, the army sent Colonel Richard Mason to check out the rumors and write a report. He found thousands of miners panning for gold in the American River. Mason estimated that about 4,000 miners were finding a total of $30,000 to $50,000 per day in gold.

Mason's report had an immediate effect on soldiers stationed at Los Angeles. Army records show that 716 enlisted men deserted between July 1, 1848, and December 31, 1849. "Laboring men at the mines can now earn in one day more than double a soldier's pay and allowances for a month," Mason stated in his report.

On August 8, 1848, a St. Louis newspaper reported that gold was being "collected at random and without any trouble" on the American River. Other major newspapers printed similar reports.

President Polk confirmed the discovery of gold in a message to Congress on December 5. "The accounts of the abundance of gold in that territory are of such an extraordinary character as would scarcely command belief were they not corroborated by the authentic reports of officers in the public service ..."

Newspapers printed the President's words along with exaggerated reports of how easy it was to find gold nuggets. The following was reported on December 6,1848, by the Hartford *Daily Courant:*

> *"The California gold fever is approaching its crisis ... By a sudden and accidental discovery, the ground is represented to be one vast gold mine. Gold is picked up in pure lumps, twenty-four carats fine. Soldiers are deserting their ranks, sailors their ships, and everybody their employment, to speed to the region of the gold mines."*

### Did You Know?
The California Legislature passed a foreign miner's tax. Miners who were not U.S. citizens had to pay a monthly fee of $20 for the right to mine for gold.

Name: _____ Date: _____

# The Forty-Niners (cont.)

## Critical Thinking

How would you have felt about going to California if you had read the newspaper reports of the gold being found? Would you have been tempted? Give specific details or examples to support your answer.

_____

_____

_____

_____

_____

## Graphic Organizer

**Directions:** Complete the vocabulary chart by creating a definition, using the word in a sentence and drawing an illustration that helps you remember the meaning of the word.

| Word | Definition | Illustration |
|------|------------|--------------|
| **forty-niner** | | |
| | Sentence | |

## Research

**Directions:** Those who rushed to the gold fields in California were also called "Argonauts of '49." The term Argonauts referred to people from Greek mythology who sailed on the ship the *Argo.* Learn more about the adventures of the mythical Argonauts. Use your research to answer the following questions.

1. For what were the Argonauts searching? _____

2. Why do you think those who went to California in search of gold were called Argonauts?

_____

_____

_____

_____

# Travel to the Gold Fields

The **migration** to the gold fields resulted in nearly 100,000 people arriving in 1849. Many thousands more followed in the next few years. There were three main modes of transportation to California.

## Wagon Train

In April of 1849, 20,000 people set out in wagon trains for the gold fields of California. Most trails to the West began at **Independence** or **St. Joseph, Missouri,** or **Council Bluffs, Iowa**. There was never one single trail to California but rather several major routes with variations. **The Oregon Trail, Santa Fe Trail,** and **California Trail** were the three most commonly used.

Those traveling with wagon trains had to take routes that were not the most direct because of several natural obstacles: the canyons of Colorado, the Sierra Nevada Mountains, and the deserts around the Great Salt Lake.

## Stagecoach

Between 1850 and 1900, stagecoaches carried tens of thousands of passengers on regularly-scheduled routes across the West. Many prospective miners chose this method of travel because it was much quicker than traveling with a wagon train. Compared to modern transportation, however, a stagecoach trip was painfully uncomfortable and dreadfully slow. The trip from Missouri to California took about a month and cost $200.

---

**Think About It**

Would you have been willing to ride 2,000 miles on a stagecoach to reach the gold fields?

---

## Clipper Ship

Many **prospectors** decided to reach California by booking passage on clipper ships. The trip around **Cape Horn** was long, dangerous, and expensive. This journey took about 100 days if everything went well. Strong currents, icebergs, and fierce winds off Cape Horn often caused ships to go off course, adding more time to the journey.

Greedy ship captains signed up as many passengers as they could crowd onto a ship. People often slept three to a bed. The supply of ships did not nearly meet the demand for travel, and many older ships that were barely seaworthy were brought into service. Once ships reached California, the crews often deserted to join the Gold Rush. Ships were abandoned and left to rot.

A second option was to sail across the Gulf of Mexico to Panama. From there, travelers walked or rode horses 100 miles through dense jungles to Panama City in the hopes of catching a ship heading north on the Pacific side. This route was also uncertain, long, and dangerous. The food was terrible, and the water was thick, murky, and often filled with insects. Yellow fever, malaria, dysentery, and cholera prevented many prospective miners from reaching California.

Name: _____  Date: _____

# Travel to the Gold Fields (cont.)

## Research

**Directions:** Thousands of prospective miners traveled to the gold fields by wagon train, stagecoach, or clipper ship. They faced many hardships on the way west. Learn more about these methods of travel. Create a study aid to organize the information using the steps below.

Step #1: Fold a sheet of white paper in half like a hotdog bun.

Step #2: Fold the paper in thirds, from side to side.

Step #3: Unfold the paper and cut up the front two folds.

Step #4: On the front of the flaps, write the methods of travel.

Step #5: Under the flaps, list the hardships travelers would experience.

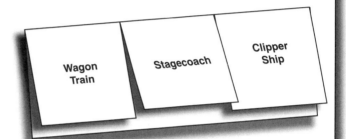

## Research

**Directions:** Yellow fever, malaria, dysentery, and cholera prevented many prospective miners traveling across Panama from reaching California. Select one of the diseases to research. Using the information, create a prospector's health pamphlet outlining the symptoms, precautions, and treatments for the disease.

## Graphic Organizer

**Directions:** Complete the vocabulary chart by creating a definition, using the word in a sentence and drawing an illustration that helps you remember the meaning of the word.

| Word | Definition | Illustration |
|------|------------|--------------|
| **migration** | | |
| | Sentence | |
| Word | Definition | Illustration |
| **prospector** | | |
| | Sentence | |

Name: _____ Date: _____

# Travel to the Gold Fields (cont.)

**Activity**

**Directions:** This song describes the hardships and dangers of the trip to California. Select one verse. On a separate sheet of paper, rewrite the verse in your own words and explain what it means.

### The Fools of Forty-Nine

When gold was found in forty-eight, the people said 'twas gas,
And some were fools enough to think the lumps were made of brass,
But they soon were satisfied and started off to mine,
They bought a ship came round the Horn in the fall of forty-nine.

    **CHORUS:**      Then they thought of what they had been told,
                        When they started after gold,
                        That they never in this world would make a pile.

The poor, the old, the rotten scows were advertised to sail
From New Orleans with passengers, but they must pump and bail.
The ships were crowded more than full, but some hung on behind,
And others dived off from the wharf and swam till they were blind.

**REPEAT CHORUS**

With rusty pork and stinking beef and rotten wormy bread
With captains too that never were as high as the mainmast head,
The steerage passengers would rave and swear they'd paid their passage
They wanted something more to eat besides Bologna sausage.

**REPEAT CHORUS**

And they begun to cross the plains with oxen, holler and 'haw;
And steamers they began to run as far as Panama,
And there for months the people stayed that started after gold,
And some returned disgusted with the lies they had been told.

**REPEAT CHORUS**

The people died on every route, they sickened and died like sheep,
And those at sea before they were dead were launched into the deep,
And those that died crossing the Plains fared not as well as that,
For a hole was dug and they was dumped along the terrible Platte.

**REPEAT CHORUS**

Name: _____ Date: _____

# Arriving at the Gold Fields

It might be difficult for people today to understand why men left homes, businesses, and families to travel thousands of miles in search of gold.

The possibility of finding a huge fortune must have been very tempting to farmers who made only two or three hundred dollars during a good year. The same was true for factory workers who made about a dollar for working a twelve-hour day.

Even skilled craftsmen made only about a dollar and a half a day. Many felt it was worth taking the chance to travel to California, where gold was free to anyone who could find it.

Stories of miners becoming rich in a short time spread like wildfire. Many of these stories were exaggerations; however, some of them were actually true.

When prospectors finally arrived in California, conditions were not what they expected. For one thing, gold nuggets weren't simply sitting around waiting to be picked up.

Another big shock was the prices merchants charged for goods. Pans needed to search for gold would have cost 20 cents before 1849. Instead, they sold for $8! The price of a horse went from $6 to over $300. Food prices were also **inflated**. A loaf of bread cost $2; a pound of butter, $6; a tin of sardines, $16; and one egg, $3!

## Critical Thinking

Why do you think merchants were able to charge such outrageous prices and get away with it? Give specific details and examples to support your answer.

_____

_____

_____

_____

## Graphic Organizer

**Directions:** Complete the vocabulary chart by creating a definition, using the word in a sentence and drawing an illustration that helps you remember the meaning of the word.

| Word | Definition | Illustration |
|------|------------|--------------|
| **inflation** | | |
| | Sentence | |

Name: _____     Date: _____

# What Miners Wore

**Shirts:** Most miners wore a basic cotton work shirt. This type of shirt is still available at many stores today. Miners also wore red wool under-shirts, winter and summer.

**Pants:** Miners, like other working men of the day, primarily wore cotton duck (canvas) or wool pants that came in different styles. The "drop front" design was popular since zippers hadn't been invented yet.

**Belts:** Although pants didn't have belt loops until the late 1800s, a miner usually wore a belt. This was not to hold up his pants, but rather as a place to hang items to keep them handy, like a pistol, knife, or gold pouch.

**Boots:** Miners bought the best leather boots they could afford. Good boots were needed as protection from sharp rocks, mud, and water. Miners were particularly thankful for good boots when a pick or shovel landed on a foot instead of rock.

**Scarves:** A large triangular cotton "kerchief" was also an essential part of every miner's costume.

**Rubberized clothing:** By 1849, a process was used to coat cloth with rubber. Rubber hat covers, raincoats, and blankets helped keep miners dry in most weather.

**Beaver Felt Low Topper**

**Hats:** Hats were essential for miners who spent many hours outside in the hot sun or cold rain. No one style was preferred, but common styles included the topper hat and the Panama hat.

**Palm Leaf Panama**

## Critical Thinking

1.  If you had been a miner, which type of hat would you have preferred? Why? Give specific details or examples to explain your answer.

    _____

    _____

    _____

    _____


3.  List several uses for a miner's kerchief. _____

    _____

    _____

    _____

Name: _____ Date: _____

# Tools of the Miner

**Canteens:** Miners usually chose metal canteens made of tin and covered in **buckskin** or cloth because they were lighter than wooden canteens.

**Lamps:** Miners could purchase candle holders (open or enclosed) or oil lamps to provide light. Candles and lamp oil were very expensive.

**Pouches:** Most miners kept their gold dust or nuggets in a soft leather pouch. The pouch was quite long, so one end could be tucked securely through the belt.

**Scales:** Many miners carried portable scales to accurately measure their daily "take" and to assure that they were not being cheated when they exchanged their gold dust and nuggets for money.

**Picks:** Miners used picks to break up rocks and hard clumps of dirt.

**Shovels:** Shovels came in a variety of shapes, sizes, and styles. The most popular shovel during the Gold Rush era was the Ames shovel made in North Eaton, Massachusetts.

**Cookware and eating utensils:** Miners carried only the bare essentials for cooking and eating. Meals were prepared in a metal pot. A tin pot for coffee or tea, a metal fork and knife, a tin plate to eat from, and a sturdy tin cup were all a miner needed to cook and eat meals.

**Matching**

_____ 1. pick

_____ 2. scale

_____ 3. buckskin

_____ 4. canteen

_____ 5. pouch

a. used to store the miner's gold dust or nuggets

b. a soft suede leather made from a deerskin or animal pelt

c. used to break up rocks and hard clumps of dirt

d. used to carry water

e. used to accurately measure the miner's daily "take"

**Fill in the Blanks**

1. The most popular shovel during the Gold Rush era was the _____ shovel made in North Eaton, Massachusetts.

2. Many miners carried portable scales to assure that they were not being _____ when they exchanged their gold dust and nuggets for money.

3. Miners carried only the bare _____ for cooking and eating.

4. The miner's gold dust pouch was quite long so one end could be tucked securely through the _____.

5. _____ and lamp _____ used for light by the miners were very expensive.

Name: _____ Date: _____

# Panning for Gold

Most early prospectors used a technique called **panning** to search for gold. The advantage of this method was that the cost of the equipment needed was minimal. As you read about panning for gold, note the disadvantages of this method and write them at the bottom of the page.

To pan for gold, a prospector had to kneel or stand at the side of or in a stream of running water. He reached down to the bottom of the stream with his pan and filled it about half full of dirt and gravel. Those without metal pans used baskets, tin cups, old hats, or blankets.

After he removed twigs and sticks from the pan, he let the pan fill with water. As he pulled the pan near the surface, he shook it back and forth, tapping it against the heel of his hand. He then tilted the edge of the pan back and forth to allow a small amount of gravel to slip over the edge. He repeated this several times until the smallest amount of debris remained. At this point, he may have spotted a flake or two of gold in the pan. When the pan contained almost no gravel, he swirled it gently. Because gold is much heavier than sand,

it stays in the center while the sand moves to the outside.

Usually the pan yielded nothing but sand, but sometimes a miner could pick out a few specks of gold. To have any chance of finding even a small amount of gold, prospectors repeated this process over and over and over, from daybreak to dark, in good weather and bad.

As more and more miners arrived to search for gold, other methods were introduced that were more effective and faster than panning for gold.

## Critical Thinking

What are the disadvantages of the panning method? Give specific details or examples to support your answer.

_____

_____

_____

_____

## Research

**Directions:** Research techniques used in panning for gold. Use this information to practice what you have learned. Place gold painted rocks of various sizes in the bottom of a child's plastic swimming pool. Cover the rocks with a layer of sand, and fill the pool with cold water. Using a metal pie pan, practice your panning techniques.

Name: _____ Date: _____

# Rocking the Cradle

Panning for gold was slow, tedious, and not very effective. Prospectors wanted a faster way to gather the gold; some decided to try another technique.

When they found a likely place on the river, miners built a **rocker**. A rocker looked something like a baby cradle with a handle on one side. The rocker was made of two shallow wooden boxes, one on top of the other.

The upper box was about half as long as the lower one and had holes in it. The lower box had cleats called riffles across it and a hole at one end. Miners shoveled sand, silt, and gravel into the top box. Then they scooped up water and poured it over the top while they rocked the cradle (moved the rocker back and forth with the handle).

The rocking motion caused pebbles that were too large to fit through the holes to remain in the upper box. Mud and water ran through the holes into and out of the lower box. The cleats caught and held any particles of gold.

This method was most effective when two people worked together; while one shoveled in the material, the other poured in the water and rocked the box.

**True or False?**

Circle "T" for true or "F" for false.

1   T   F   Using a rocker was faster than panning for gold.

2.   T   F   Two people were needed to use a rocker.

3.   T   F   The lower box of the rocker was shorter than the upper one.

4.   T   F   When the miner pulled the handle, all the rocks and pebbles in the upper box fell out.

5.   T   F   The cleats in the lower box kept particles of gold from washing away.

UNIT THREE: GOLD RUSH

# Using a Long Tom

Another method of searching for gold was to build a **long tom**. This also consisted of wooden boxes on two levels. Each box was about a foot and a half wide and about eight feet long. Both had one open end covered with a strainer. The closed ends were raised several inches higher than the open ends. Like rockers, the boxes had cleats or riffles that formed grooves or ridges to catch and hold gold particles.

To use a long tom, miners needed a constant source of running water. They could dig a trough to divert the water from a stream to the long tom or use pipes or hoses.

It took three people to work the long tom effectively. Two people shoveled muck from the river or stream into the top box, while a third person constantly stirred the muck to keep it from clogging up. As the material was washed away by the running water, small particles of gold could be caught in the cleats.

## Did You Know?

Between 1848 and 1856, about 465 million dollars worth of gold was discovered in California. However, geologists have confirmed that the majority of the gold is still there; as much as 85 percent of the gold remains. Each year, new veins are exposed as many geological changes take place, such as floods, earthquakes, droughts, freezing temperatures, and mud slides.

## True or False

Circle "T" for true or "F" for false.

1. T   F   It took five people to work the long tom effectively.
2. T   F   The majority of the gold that ever was in California is still there.
3. T   F   Geological changes such as floods, earthquakes, droughts, freezing temperatures, and mud slides can expose veins of gold.
4. T   F   Miners liked to use a long tom because they did not need a source of running water.
5. T   F   The long tom consisted of wooden boxes on two levels.

Name: _____ Date: _____

# Sluicing for Gold

A **sluice** was similar to a long tom, except that it contained more wooden boxes and could be several hundred feet long. A sluice needed to be built across a sharp bend in a stream or river to connect the two parts of the stream and make the water detour across the riffles.

The miners shoveled dirt and gravel into the highest box and let the water wash it out of the sluice. Like rocker boxes and long toms, the riffles in the sluice caught the small particles of gold

## Critical Thinking

If you had been a "forty-niner," which method would you have preferred: using a rocker box, a long tom, a sluice, or panning for gold? Why? Give specific details and examples to support your answer.

_____

_____

_____

_____

_____

## Graphic Organizer

**Directions:** Prospectors used several different techniques in their search for gold. Using the information on pages 98–101, create a study aid to display the information about each mining technique.

Step #1: Place four sheets of white paper in a stack. Layer the sheets one on top of the other so each has a bottom border of one-half inch.

Step #2: Fold the stack of paper in half.

Step #3: Crease the fold and staple across the top.

Step #4: Write the title on the first page and label the tabs as shown in the illustration at the right.

Step #5: Write what you have learned about each technique under the correct tab.

Prospecting for Gold

Pan

Rocker

Long Tom

Sluice

UNIT THREE: GOLD RUSH

Name: _____ Date: _____

# Gold Rush Towns: **Shantytowns and Boomtowns**

Whenever a quantity of gold was discovered in a new area, hundreds rushed there to try their luck. Small communities sprang up almost overnight. Miners lived in tents and rickety shacks, called shanties. If there wasn't much gold in the area, the "shantytown" disappeared as quickly as it began, often even before it had been named.

If the gold strike was a big one, a "boomtown" grew quickly. Homes and buildings for doctors, bankers, blacksmiths, and merchants sprang up among the tents and shacks. Many small towns boomed for a time during the California Gold Rush but then were deserted once the gold played out in the area.

The biggest, wildest boomtown in California was San Francisco. The population increased by 25,000 in two years. At one time, an average of 30 houses a day were being built. Besides homes, businesses, saloons, and gambling houses sprang up.

Although San Francisco continued to flourish after the Gold Rush, many boomtowns were deserted. Abandoned boomtowns soon became ghost towns. Remains of some of these towns have become popular tourist attractions.

Of the thousands of mining camps that arose during the years of the Gold Rush, most have disappeared without a trace. Towns like Hell-out-for-Noon City, Slumgullion, Delirium Tremens, Bogus Thunder, Graveyard, Mugfuzzle Flat, and Hell's Delight are only memories from diaries, newspapers, and maps.

---

**Think About It**

Why do you think miners lived in tents and shanties rather than building nice homes?

---

## Extension Activity

**Directions:** Select one of the gold rush towns listed below. On a separate sheet of paper, write a short story about how the town might have gotten its name. Remember, a story should have a beginning, middle, and ending.

| | | | | |
|---|---|---|---|---|
| Downieville | Sierra City | Truckee | Ponderosa | Camptonville |
| North Bloomfield | French Corral | Washington | Bridgeport | Dutch Flat |
| Rough & Ready | Nevada City | Gold Run | Grass Valley | Iowa Hill |
| Foresthill | Georgetown | Auburn | Pilot Hill | Lotus |
| Placerville | Diamond Springs | El Dorado | Fiddletown | Shingle Springs |
| Drytown | Volcano | Railroad Flat | Butte City | Campo Seco |
| Mokelumne Hill | Mountain Ranch | San Andreas | Jenny Lind | Douglas Flat |
| Calaveritas | Vallecito | Copperopolis | Angels Camp | Fourth Crossing |
| Sonora | Columbia | Carson Hill | Jackass Hill | Montezuma |
| Chinese Camp | Double Springs | Crimea House | Big Oak Flat | Knights Ferry |
| Groveland | Coulterville | Bagby | Bear Valley | Mariposa |
| Mt. Ophir | Hornitos | Agua Fria | Oakhurst | Plymouth |

Name: _____  Date: _____

# Staking a Claim

Until gold was discovered in California, there were no laws regarding mining. As the forty-niners rushed to the area, a series of informal **codes** was established in mining camps.

When a miner found traces of gold, he could stake a **claim** to the area. This gave him the exclusive right to search for gold there, but it did not give him ownership of the land. Claims were limited to one per person. If no one worked a claim for a week, it became available to anyone else who wanted to claim it.

The size of a claim varied. In some mining camps, a claim was limited to 10 square feet. In others, the limit was 50 square feet. "**Jumping**" a claim (taking over someone else's claim by force) happened frequently.

Claims officers were paid by miners. They patrolled the area, settled disputes, and oversaw the buying and selling of sites. Sometimes swindlers "**salted**" a claim. They scattered a small amount of gold dust in the dirt and then sold their claims for large amounts of money. Where no mining camps existed, miners tried to claim large areas of land. However, if word of a gold strike leaked out, it was impossible for one person to defend a large area.

**Think About It**
Why do you think people salted claims?

## Matching

_____ 1. stake a claim
_____ 2. codes
_____ 3. salt a claim
_____ 4. jump a claim

a. to scatter a small amount of gold dust in the dirt
b. miner marks an area of land and declares rights to any gold found there
c. informal rules
d. to take over someone's claim by force

## Constructed Response

Explain why it was in the miners' best interest to follow the codes in mining camps even if they weren't legally enforced. Give specific details or examples to support your answer.

_____

_____

_____

_____

## Cooperative Learning

**Directions:** To visualize the size of a claim, imagine the sidewalk is a stream. Each member of the class marks an area equal to 10 square feet along both sides of the sidewalk and stands in their "claim."

Name: _____ Date: _____

# Getting Rich

Early in the California Gold Rush, prospectors could expect to find about an ounce of gold in creeks and rivers on a given day. Since gold was worth $16 an ounce, this didn't amount to a fortune for most miners. Although reports of the amount of gold available and the number of big strikes were exaggerated, many miners did become very wealthy.

Some California miners accomplished what they set out to do—they struck it rich and took home a fortune. Those lucky few paid off mortgages on their farms and started new lives.

Not everyone who got rich during the California Gold Rush did it by mining for gold, however. Some gave up mining but stayed in California to open businesses in the boomtowns or to farm the fertile valleys.

Two men who got their start in the boomtowns of California were Levi Strauss and Philip Armour.

**Philip Armour**

Strauss sold trousers made of sturdy cotton denim to the miners. Armour made his fortune by opening a butcher shop and supplying meat to the miners. His business grew until he eventually became the largest supplier of beef in the United States.

Some made money in other ways. Gamblers found it was easier to extract gold from the pockets of gullible miners than to dig for it in the gold fields. Con men sold useless items at inflated prices.

In 1849, merchants charged miners outlandish prices for supplies and services. Sugar sold for $2 a pound, and coffee was $4 a pound. Men and women earned $50 a week doing laundry. Restaurants charged $25 or more for meals. Successful miners could easily pay them, but many miners could barely make ends meet.

**Levi Strauss**

## Research

**Directions:** Find out more about the lives of Levi Strauss and Philip Armour. Create a study aid to organize the information.

1. Fold a sheet of white paper hotdog style. Fold the paper so the back is one-half inch taller than the front. Write the title in this space.
2. Fold the paper in thirds, from side to side.
3. Unfold the paper and draw a Venn diagram on the front flap as shown.
4. Cut down the front two folds.
5. On the front of the flaps write one man's name in the first circle and the other man's name in the last circle. Write the word Both in the center circle.

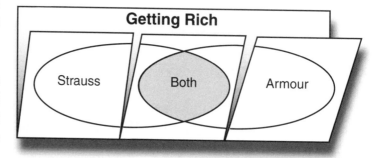
**Getting Rich**

Strauss    Both    Armour

Name: _____ Date: _____

# Women Strike It Rich

Although men were the ones first infected with gold fever, women caught it, too. When women began arriving in California, they were welcomed enthusiastically, since the overwhelming majority of the first wave of prospectors were men. Some women tried mining for gold, but most found they could make as much as or more than most miners by using their practical skills.

Any woman who could cook was able to earn money serving food with a minimum of equipment. A board across a pair of sawhorses could serve as a table. If she didn't have enough cups, plates, or silverware, the miners shared.

If a woman could bake biscuits, bread, cakes, or pies, fry steak and eggs, or make stew or soup, she was almost guaranteed more customers than she could handle. Even with the high cost of ingredients, miners were willing to pay for "home-cooked" meals.

Other women found they could earn good money by sewing, mending, washing, ironing, and cleaning. Some women ran **boardinghouses** or hotels. The census of 1850 showed 23 women living in Nevada City, California. Of them, 12 took in boarders or ran hotels with their husbands, and three others worked in family taverns that took in boarders.

At that time, many people believed that women had a "civilizing" influence on men. When women lived in a community, schools, churches, and benevolent societies were soon established.

California was the first state to allow women to own property in their own name. (In other states, everything a woman had before marriage or earned afterwards belonged to her husband.) This encouraged many women to settle in California.

## True or False

**Directions:** Circle "T" for true or "F" for false.

1. T   F   Miners were willing to pay high prices for "home-cooked" meals.
2. T   F   The census of 1850 showed 100 women living in Nevada City, California.
3. T   F   California was the last state to allow women to own property in their own name.
4. T   F   The overwhelming majority of the first wave of prospectors were young, single women looking to strike it rich.
5. T   F   Cooking was a skill women used to make money during the California Gold Rush.

Name: _____ Date: _____

# Prices: Then and Now

Food prices in the gold fields of California were much higher than anywhere else in the United States at that time.

**Activity**

1. **Directions:** Compare the prices of these items during the Gold Rush to prices today. Calculate the difference between then and now.

| ITEM | GOLD RUSH PRICES | PRICES TODAY | DIFFERENCE |
|---|---|---|---|
| Bread | $2/loaf (At restaurants, bread sold for $1 a slice.) | | |
| Butter | $6/pound | | |
| Cheese | $8/pound | | |
| Onions | $1.50/pound | | |
| Tin of Sardines | $16 each | | |
| Eggs | $3 each ($36 a dozen) | | |
| Flour | $1/pound | | |
| Coffee | $4/pound | | |
| Dried Beans | $1/pound | | |
| Sugar | $2/pound | | |

2. **Directions:** For each shopping list below, calculate the cost then and now.

**List A:**  1# cheese
1# butter
1 loaf of bread
1# beans
Total then: _____
Total now: _____

**List B:**  5# flour
1 dozen eggs
1 tin of sardines
2# coffee
2# onions
Total then: _____
Total now: _____

Name: _____ Date: _____

# The Lousy Miner

**Extension Activity**

**Directions:** This song, sung during the Gold Rush years, tells much about the life of unsuccessful miners. On your own paper, rewrite each verse in your own words. (Hint: *Lousy* has more than one meaning.)

### The Lousy Miner

It's four long years since I reached this land,
In search of gold among the rocks and sand;
And yet I'm poor when the truth is told.
　　I'm a lousy miner,
　　I'm a lousy miner in search of shining gold.

I've lived on swine till I grunt and squeal,
No one can tell how my bowels feel,
With slapjacks a-swimming in bacon grease.
　　I'm a lousy miner,
　　I'm a lousy miner in search of shining gold.

I was covered with lice coming on the boat,
I threw away my fancy swallow-tailed coat,
And now they crawl up and down my back.
　　I'm a lousy miner,
　　I'm a lousy miner in search of shining gold.

My sweetheart vowed she'd wait for me
Till I returned; but don't you see
She's married now, sure, so I'm told,
　　Left her lousy miner,
　　Left her lousy miner, in search of shining gold.

Oh, land of gold, you did me deceive,
And I intend in thee my bones to leave;
So farewell home, now I grow cold,
　　I'm a lousy miner,
　　I'm a lousy miner in search of shining gold.

**UNIT THREE: GOLD RUSH**

Name: _____ Date: _____

# Gold Rush Justice

Most types of gold mining required the cooperation of two or more people. People formed **partnerships** to build and operate rockers, long toms, and sluices. Arguments arose over how to split the **profits**. Many disputes ended in fights or even murder.

There were no official law enforcement agents in the gold fields of California. At the height of the Gold Rush, about two murders a day were committed in San Francisco alone.

California was part of Mexico until the end of the Mexican War in 1848. Although the area was legally administered by the U.S. Army after that, there was no formal government until California became a state in 1850. Even then people were more interested in prospecting than in becoming part of a legal system that would take time away from their search for gold.

As soon as word of a new gold strike leaked out, hundreds of miners rushed to the area. They staked nearby claims, hoping to collect a share of the wealth. Sometimes the person who had staked the original claim was murdered, and others took over the claim.

The Gold Rush town of **Bodie**, high in the Sierras, gained a reputation as the most lawless mining town in the West. The local newspaper even published a column titled "Last Night's Killings."

In many cases, people took the law into their own hands. Without courts, lawyers, judges, and juries, justice wasn't always fair; it could be swift and merciless. When **vigilante** groups captured someone accused of a crime, he might be punished without a trial.

Robbery also became a major problem. Not only did people steal gold, they also stole equipment, firewood, horses, and even food from each other. In 1851, the California legislature passed a law allowing the death penalty for stealing property worth more than $100. **Banishment**, cutting off a person's ears, branding, and whipping, as well as hanging, were common forms of punishment.

## Matching

_____ 1. vigilante

_____ 2. banishment

_____ 3. Bodie

_____ 4. partnership

_____ 5. profit

a. exile

b. a member of a group who illegally punishes a criminal

c. two or more individuals combine resources to form a business

d. money left over after a business pays expenses

e. most lawless mining town in the West

## Critical Thinking

Greed was the dominant motive for crimes during the California Gold Rush. Do you agree or disagree with this statement? On your own paper, explain your answer using specific details or examples.

UNIT THREE: GOLD RUSH

Name: _____ Date: _____

# "The Wickedest Town in the West"

High in the Sierras, summers are cool. Rain is rare except for occasional violent thunderstorms. Winters bring strong winds, subzero temperatures, and 20 feet of snow. Not much grows there other than sagebrush. Although it is not a sunny California town, over 10,000 people once lived in Bodie, California.

In the fall of 1859, Bill Bodey began exploring for gold in the area with three partners. One story claims Bodey chased a wounded rabbit into a hole. While trying to get at the rabbit, he discovered gold.

The partners knew how treacherous winter could be, so they decided to wait until the following spring to work the claim. Bodey couldn't wait. He and another man returned, built a cabin, and continued to explore the area.

In November, the two men were caught in a blizzard. His partner made it back to the cabin, but Bodey didn't. His body wasn't found until the following spring.

Rich strikes in places with better weather drew attention away from Bodie for a time. Then in 1876, a rich vein of gold was discovered, and the rush to Bodie began. By the following year, the town had grown to 2,000. Another gold strike in 1878 caused the population to swell to over 10,000. Crime increased as quickly as the population of Bodie.

With so many people arriving so quickly, nearly everything was in short supply. Because of its location, all supplies, including lumber and firewood, had to be brought in by freight wagons. At times, the severe weather prevented anyone from getting into or out of the area for long periods.

After a long series of assaults, robberies, and murders, citizens of the city decided enough was enough. On January 14, 1881, a mob lynched a man accused of murder. From then on, the vigilante group kept some semblance of order in the town that had earned the nickname "the wickedest town in the West."

Today, Bodie is a California state historic park. Only tourists wander down Main Street now. The deserted buildings are silent and so is the cemetery where so many dreams are buried.

**UNIT THREE: GOLD RUSH**

---

**Extension Activity**

Imagine that you have recently arrived in California from the east coast after a long, difficult journey that lasted almost a year. Hearing about the gold found in Bodie, your family decides to continue on and settle there. You've heard about the weather and the crime in Bodie, as well as the stories of fantastic amounts of gold found there.

**Directions:** On a separate sheet of paper, write a letter to a friend telling how you feel about moving to Bodie, California. Use the friendly letter format. Give specific details or examples to explain your feelings about the move.

---

Name: _____ Date: _____

# Black Bart

One of California's better-known Gold Rush villains, Charles E. Bolton (**a.k.a.** Black Bart), was responsible for 28 Wells Fargo stagecoach robberies.

Black Bart was born in England in 1829 and moved with his parents to upstate New York at the age of two. His real name was Charles Bowles, which he later changed to Boles. After making several trips to California to prospect during the early years of the Gold Rush, he married and settled in Illinois on a farm. He fought for the Union in the Civil War. After the war, he moved to Montana to try gold mining again, but was forced off his claim by the Wells Fargo company. He was also a peddler of **patent medicines** before turning to robbery.

Black Bart's first hold-up in 1875 near Copperopolis wasn't very profitable. The **strongbox** contained only $160.

Stories about Black Bart claimed he never robbed individual passengers. He was nicknamed "the gentleman bandit" because he said "please" and "thank you" when robbing a stage. He even politely called the driver "Sir."

Black Bart soon became a celebrity in local newspapers. When he left his first bit of poetry in an emptied strongbox, he became a legend.

**Charles E. Bolton
(a.k.a. "Black Bart")**

For a time, authorities couldn't find any clues to Black Bart's identity. He wore a flour sack over his head and a full-length linen **duster** during robberies.

Black Bart eluded captivity until 1883 when he cut his hand trying to open a strongbox. Distracted by an approaching rider, he dropped the handkerchief he was using to wipe off the blood. The **laundry mark** on the handkerchief led investigators to Charles E. Bolton of San Francisco.

When he was finally arrested, people were surprised to learn he was 54 years old. They also discovered that his shotgun hadn't even contained shells when he robbed the stagecoaches.

## Think About It

Why do you think people make heroes out of people who are criminals?

## Matching

_____ 1. a.k.a.

_____ 2. patent medicine

_____ 3. strongbox

_____ 4. duster

_____ 5. laundry mark

a. tag or stamp left by the laundry that last cleaned the item

b. long coat worn to protect the clothes from dust

c. also known as

d. a strongly made chest or case for storing money or valuables

e. nonprescription drug that is protected by a trademark but whose ingredients are not fully listed; usually claimed to cure many ailments, but without any proof

# San Francisco

**San Francisco** was only a sleepy village on the Pacific coast before the Gold Rush. It grew from about 800 people in 1848, to 15,000 by 1849, and 25,000 one year later, becoming one of the fastest-growing cities in the world. By 1856, San Francisco had more than 50,000 citizens and was the largest and most important city in the West.

Ships carrying merchandise, supplies, and miners to California usually landed in San Francisco. Gold being shipped back east went out through that city. Miners bought their supplies, banked their gold, collected their mail, and came for recreation and relaxation. San Francisco had it all.

When cities grow quickly, they tend to be crowded, dirty, and poorly planned. San Francisco was no exception. From a field of canvas tents and wooden shacks, a town of houses and businesses grew almost overnight. **Prefabricated** houses shipped to San Francisco could be assembled in a day.

Abandoned ships clogged the harbor, deserted by their crews who ran off to hunt for gold. Material from some ships was scavenged for building. Many of the ships simply rotted away in the harbor.

Most streets were unpaved, and few had sidewalks. When it rained, mud and potholes made some streets impassable. A terrible fire broke out in May 1851; in just ten hours, it destroyed 2,000 homes and much of the business district.

Gradually new buildings of brick replaced the wooden ones. Places for rent were vastly overpriced. Labor was **scarce**. Wages were high and so was the cost of living. The price of houses skyrocketed to $75,000. The price of food, supplies, and services increased as much as 1,000 percent.

Rats infested the city. Cats sold for $16 each. Robberies were common. Most men carried weapons for protection, especially after dark on the unlit streets. Saloons became the social centers of the city, where people conducted business, drank, gambled, and were entertained by musicians and dancers.

Almost anyone willing to work could find a way to make money in San Francisco at that time.

Name: _____ Date: _____

# San Francisco (cont.)

**Directions:** Complete the following activities.

**Fill in the Blanks**

1. Ships carrying merchandise, supplies, and miners to California usually landed in

   _____ _____.

2. Abandoned ships clogged the San Francisco harbor, deserted by their crews who ran off
   to hunt for _____.

3. Material from some ships was _____ for building.

4. During the Gold Rush, _____ in San Francisco became the social
   centers of the city.

5. By 1856, San Francisco had more than 50,000 citizens and was the largest and most
   important city in the _____.

**True or False**
**Directions:** Circle "T" for true or "F" for false.

1. T   F   Almost anyone willing to work could find a way to make money in San Francisco
           during the Gold Rush.
2. T   F   Most streets in San Francisco during the Gold Rush were paved and had
           sidewalks.
3. T   F   During the Gold Rush, prefabricated houses shipped to San Francisco could be
           assembled in a day.
4. T   F   San Francisco was the largest city on the Pacific coast before the Gold Rush.
5. T   F   In San Francisco during the Gold Rush, rent was affordable and labor was
           abundant.

**Cause and Effect**
**Directions:** A **cause** is an event that produces a result. An **effect** is the result produced or
what happens. For each cause, write an effect.

1. Cause:  Thousands of miners traveled to San Francisco in 1849.
   Effect: _____

   _____

2. Cause:  Prices in California were very high during the Gold Rush era.
   Effect: _____

   _____

3. Cause:  During the Gold Rush, San Francisco became one of the fastest-growing cities in
   the world.
   Effect: _____

   _____

Name: _____ Date: _____

# The Rest of the Story

Although James Marshall discovered the first gold on property owned by John Sutter, neither man profited from the discovery. **Squatters** overran the property Sutter had hoped to turn into an agriculture-based empire.

Sutter's 50,000 acres of land were invaded and ruined by prospectors searching for gold. They trampled his crops, muddied the streams, and killed his cattle for food.

"The country swarmed with lawless men," wrote John Sutter. "Talking with them did no good. I was alone and there was no law."

With his dreams of an agricultural empire crushed, Sutter tried his luck mining but never struck it rich. Years later he traveled to Washington, D.C., to ask Congress to recognize his claim to the land he had received from Mexico. While waiting for the decision, Sutter died in a Washington, D.C., hotel room on June 18, 1880.

James Marshall became famous for discovering gold at Sutter's Mill, but like Sutter, he never became wealthy from that discovery. He tried prospecting, but like Sutter, he never

located another rich strike. Marshall was forced to sell his own small ranch to pay off debts.

Marshall grew fruit and produced wines and brandies but failed after a few years. He tried prospecting again, bought into a partnership in a worthless mine, and even went on a lecture tour to raise money.

In 1872, the California State Legislature provided a two-year renewable pension for Marshall in recognition of his role in the state's history. Legend has it that when he went before the legislature in 1878 to ask for another renewal, a brandy bottle dropped out of his pocket, and the pension was denied. James Marshall died in poverty in 1885.

## Graphic Organizer

**Directions:** The discovery of gold by James Marshall on the property owned by John Sutter had grave consequences for both men. Fold a sheet of white paper in half like a hotdog bun. Fold the paper in half again, from side to side. Unfold the paper and cut up the fold, making two flaps. On the front flaps, write the names of the two men. Under the flaps, write how the discovery of gold affected each man's life.

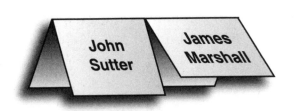

Name: _____ Date: _____

# Consequences of the Gold Rush

Before the Gold Rush of 1849, the area that became the state of California was sparsely settled. The Gold Rush transformed not only the lives of people but also California itself. California's population grew dramatically. Its towns, cities, and businesses thrived. Almost overnight, it became the most famous American state. People around the world knew the story of California, the golden land where a fortune could be dug from the ground.

Many of those who set off for California to find fame and fortune found hardship or death instead. Many never made it to California at all, dying during the 15,000-mile voyage around South America, as they crossed the jungles of Panama, or during the 2,000-mile overland trip from Missouri. Of those who did make it to California, many fell victim to disease, violence, or murder. Many of the women

and children waiting back east never saw their loved ones again or ever found out what had happened to them.

About 200,000 Native Americans lived in California before 1849. They were isolated from the rest of the United States by mountain ranges and deserts. Although many different tribes lived there, each remained separate from the others. For the most part, they were Stone Age people. They had no domesticated beasts of burden, little formal government, no metal tools, and no written language. They hunted with bows and stone-tipped arrows. They used nets, hooks, and harpoons for fishing. They also gathered grasses, herbs, nuts, roots, seeds, and berries for food.

Not all the gold found in California was taken from streams. Much of the gold in California was buried deep underground (and still is). When the forty-niners left, mining companies moved in with work crews and large machinery.

Hydraulic mining was a method used to explore for gold in the soil of older, dried riverbeds. Powerful jets of water were sprayed against the land to wash out the gold. This type of mining caused much environmental damage. The landscape was pocked and rutted; rivers were clogged with the runoff silt. Hydraulic mining was banned in 1884.

## Research

**Directions:** Select a topic related to the consequences of the Gold Rush for a presentation. Include a written report and visual aids, such as a poster, collage, graph, demonstration, or diorama.

Possible topics are:

- The environmental impact of the California Gold Rush
- The effect of the Gold Rush on one group of Native Americans in California
- The effect of the Gold Rush on the demographics of California

114

Name: _____  Date: _____

# Search for the Gold

**Directions**: Look up, down, backward, forward, and diagonally to find and circle the 30 words hidden in the puzzle.

```
G  L  D  H  W  T  S  R  S  Y  M  F  K  M  X  Z  Z  T  P
B  D  J  M  X  M  T  N  Y  X  C  L  C  N  R  X  W  C  Y
Q  C  W  J  I  T  W  F  M  O  T  G  N  O  L  S  A  I  L
L  K  Q  A  M  O  W  S  T  U  A  N  O  G  R  A  W  F  M
B  S  L  S  T  I  M  C  S  G  O  L  D  R  U  S  H  J  R
W  C  L  M  P  R  N  H  M  T  C  V  T  P  V  W  W  E  F
L  E  O  U  K  M  O  I  E  P  I  S  E  M  X  Y  N  O  K
G  O  A  H  I  V  A  G  N  G  S  H  R  K  T  I  R  P  K
B  N  Q  L  E  C  G  C  I  G  N  A  U  H  M  T  L  R  Q
V  K  I  L  T  U  E  L  V  B  W  N  T  T  U  C  L  O  V
P  V  S  N  N  H  A  C  M  K  O  T  N  N  D  I  N  S  R
I  T  F  K  N  N  Y  P  G  N  T  Y  E  T  N  L  W  P  R
C  R  R  L  T  A  Y  D  R  B  T  T  V  X  A  U  F  E  X
K  L  K  E  U  G  P  N  O  A  S  O  D  R  S  A  K  C  M
S  L  Z  W  V  C  Z  H  C  R  O  W  A  V  R  R  N  T  M
W  D  T  L  R  E  K  B  K  T  H  N  N  C  T  D  R  O  J
X  S  H  I  P  S  F  Y  E  Q  G  M  K  R  R  Y  T  R  J
L  J  B  L  L  I  M  S  R  E  T  T  U  S  J  H  N  S  P
N  W  P  N  F  O  R  T  Y  N  I  N  E  R  S  Q  N  L  Q
```

| | | | | |
|---|---|---|---|---|
| ADVENTURE | FEVER | LONG TOM | PICKS | SHIPS |
| ARGONAUTS | FORTUNE | LUCKY | PROSPECTORS | SHOVELS |
| BART | FORTY-NINERS | MINER | ROCKER | SLUICE |
| BOOMTOWNS | GHOST TOWNS | MINING | SAIL | SUTTER'S MILL |
| CLAIMS | GOLD RUSH | NUGGET | SAND | VIGILANTE |
| CAMPS | HYDRAULIC | PANNING | SHANTYTOWN | WEALTHY |

1. What sport do the 49ers play? _____

2. What city are they from? _____

Name: _____ Date: _____

# Gold Rush Research Project

**Directions:** Learn more about the California Gold Rush period of American history. Select one topic listed below for your research project. Construct a pie book to display your information. Directions for constructing the pie book can be found on the next page.

**Lola Montez**

**Samuel Brannan**

### PEOPLE
Philip Armour
Black Bart
James Beckworth
Samuel Brannan
J. Goldsborough Bruff
Louise Clappe
Lotta Crabtree
Eliza Farnham
Bret Harte
James Marshall
Lola Montez
Sarah Pellet
Levi Strauss
John Sutter
Luzena Wilson

### EVENTS AND MINING METHODS
Chinese emigrants to the goldfields
Compromise of 1850
Coyoting method
European emigrants to the goldfields
Hydraulic mining
The Mexican War
Quartz mining
Women's rights in California

**Bret Harte**

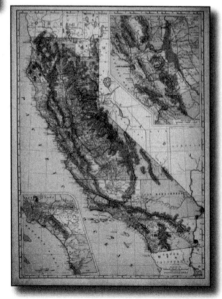

### PLACES
American River
California Trail
Carson Hill
Coloma
Fort Ross
Hangtown
Juan Fernandez Island
Lake of Gold
Nevada City, California
Sacramento
San Francisco
Sutter's Fort
Sutter's Mill

Name: _____ Date: _____

# Gold Rush Research Project (cont.)

**Directions:** Construct a pie book to display your research.

1. Cut two 12″ circles out of poster board paper. Fold both circles in quarters. Unfold them. Now, cut along one fold line to the center of the circle on both circles.

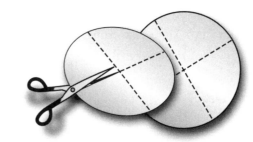

2. Starting at the slit, number the sections of one circle from 1 to 4 clockwise. Starting at the slit, number the sections of the second circle from 5 to 8 clockwise.

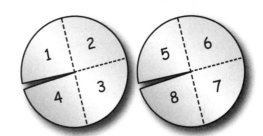

3. Place the numbered 5–8 circle on top of the numbered 1–4 circle and line up the slits.

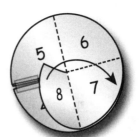

4. Pull back the #8 section and tape the #5 and #4 sections together. Fold the quarter sections counterclockwise, starting with the #8 section.

5. Fold until you have a pie slice. Organize your research information on the pages of your pie book.

# Answer Keys

(No answers are listed for activities where answers may vary.)

## Unit One: Lewis and Clark Expedition

### Lewis and Clark Time Line Activity (p. 2)

| A. | 10 | B. | 7 | C. | 3 | D. | 2 | E. | 6 |
|----|----|----|----|----|----|----|----|----|----|
| F. | 9 | G. | 8 | H. | 4 | I. | 1 | J. | 5 |

### *True or False*
1. T    2. F    3. T    4. F    5. F

### Meriwether Lewis (p. 3)
*Cause and Effect*
Possible answers include:
1. Lewis' father left home to fight against the British.
2. There were no schools in Georgia.
3. He attended school.
4. He enjoyed his experience in the militia.

### William Clark (p. 4)
1. August 1, 1770; near Richmond, Virginia
2. Virginia to Kentucky
3. natural history and science
4. hunting, fishing, tracking, camping, land navigation
5. captain
6. fought but respected the Native Americans

### Lewis and Clark (p. 5)
*Graphic Organizer*
Lewis: five years of formal schooling; naturalist; studied medicine, botany, zoology, and celestial navigation; slender build; dark hair; moody and impatient
Both: born in Virginia; skilled in hunting and fishing; over six feet tall; captains in the army
Clark: no formal schooling; geographer; mapmaker; nature artist; riverboat man; skilled in trapping and camping; stocky build; red hair; sociable and even-tempered

### The Louisiana Purchase (p. 8)
*Matching*
 1. d    2. e    3. a    4. c    5. b
*Map*
1. Louisiana, Arkansas, Missouri, Iowa, Minnesota, North Dakota, South Dakota, Nebraska, Kansas, Oklahoma, Texas, New Mexico, Colorado, Wyoming, Montana
2. Montana, Idaho, Washington, Oregon

### The Teton Sioux (p. 15)

| A. | 4 | B. | 10 | C. | 1 | D. | 3 | E. | 2 |
|----|----|----|----|----|----|----|----|----|----|
| F. | 6 | G. | 9 | H. | 5 | I. | 7 | J. | 8 |

### Sacajawea (p. 17)
*Fill in the Blanks*
1. interpreter
2. Fort Mandan
3. first born
4. war party
5. Touissaint Charbonneau

### Meeting the Shoshone (p. 18)
1. Are we not drawn onward, we few, drawn onward to new era?
2. Are we not drawn onward, we few, drawn onward to new era? (Palindrome)

### Mapping the Journey (p. 19)
Teacher check map.

### After the Expedition (p. 20)
1. $280      3. $448

### Searching for Lewis and Clark (p. 21)

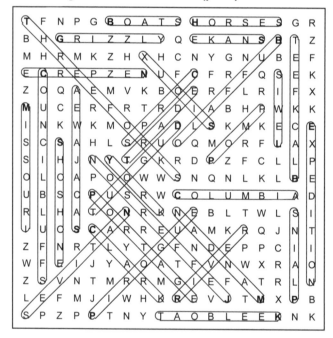

## Unit Two: Westward Expansion and Migration

### Westward Expansion and Migration Time Line Activity (p. 25)
1. Joseph Smith established the Church of Jesus Christ of Latter-day Saints.
2. The War of 1812 began.
3. Treaty of Paris
4. Mexico won independence from Spain.
5. Congress passed the Indian Removal Act.

6. Gold was discovered in California.
7. The Donner Party met disaster.
8. The transcontinental telegraph was completed.
9. John Bidwell organized the Western Emigration Society.
10. James Polk was elected president.
11. The Civil War began.
12. Andrew Jackson was elected president.
13. Mexico
14. Jim Bridger and Louis Vasquez
15. John Tyler

**Westward Movement and Expansion (p. 27)**
**Fill in the Blanks**
1. Proclamation, 1763
2. Kentucky
3. income, wealth, freedom
4. Florida, pirates
5. Canada
*Research*
The Proclamation of 1763 forbade any settlement west of the Appalachian Mountains. This was done because England feared Native American uprisings and didn't want to maintain a large army in that area to protect settlers.

**Bison (p. 36)**
*Matching*
1. c   2. e   3. b   4. a   5. d
*Fill in the Blanks*
1. buffalo
2. 2,000; 12
3. trappers, fur
4. tourists, shoot
5. Native Americans

**Narcissa and Marcus Whitman (p. 38)**
*Matching*
1. d   2. c   3. e   4. b   5. a
*Fill in the Blanks*
1. doctor, preacher
2. Henry, Eliza
3. Rocky
4. medicine, school
5. Cayuse

**Trails Led West (p. 40)**
*Matching*
1. c   2. a   3. d   4. e   5. b
*Fill in the Blanks*
1. guidebooks
2. Native Americans
3. Missouri
4. Independence, Council Bluffs
5. obstacles

**Santa Fe Trail (p. 42)**
1. Colorado
2. Colorado
3. New Mexico
4. New Mexico
5. Kansas
6. Kansas
7. Missouri
8. Colorado
9. Kansas
10. Kansas

**Oregon Fever (p. 43)**
1. F   2. T   3. F   4. F   5. F   6. F   7. F

**Oregon Trail (p. 45)**
1. Wyoming
2. Oregon
3. Nebraska
4. Nebraska
5. Wyoming
6. Idaho
7. Nebraska
8. Wyoming
9. Missouri
10. Idaho
11. Idaho
12. Oregon

**Forts Along the Trail (p. 46)**
1. Santa Fe
2. Oregon
3. Santa Fe
4. Santa Fe
5. Oregon
6. Oregon
7. Oregon
8. Santa Fe
9. Oregon
10. Oregon

**Conestoga Wagons (p. 49)**
*Fill in the Blanks*
1. Conestoga
2. 15; 20
3. expensive
4. prairie schooners
5. wheels
6. six
7. table, cupboard
8. farm
*Constructed Response*
Its purpose was to hold small tools.

**Supplying the Wagons (p. 51)**
1. $180
2. 4 oxen
3. $21
4. $6.35
5. 10 pounds of beans
6. 50 cents
7. Nails had to be transported to Oregon or made from metal that was transported.

**Wagon Trains (p. 53)**
*Matching*
1. c   2. d   3. a   4. e   5. b
*Fill in the Blanks*
1. wagon train, 50
2. leaders, laws
3. weight
4. supplies
5. dawn
*Constructed Response*
advantage: less dusty
disadvantage: had to be ready to roll earlier than the others

**What Is It? (p. 54)**
1. Ox yoke: used to control a pair of oxen
2. Horseshoe: used to protect horses' feet
3. Razor strop: used to sharpen razors for shaving
4. Whetstone: used to sharpen knives, axes, etc.
5. Wagon jack: used to help remove, repair, and replace wagon wheels
6. Wheel rim: iron band placed around a wooden wheel for strength
7. Spinning wheel: used to spin thread or yarn
8. Wooden barrel: used to store water, flour, and other items

**Children on the Trail (p. 57)**
*Matching*
1. d   2. a   3. b   4. c   5. e
*Fill in the Blanks*
1. adopted
2. Bible
3. lighten
4. plants, bison
5. bushels

**The Donner Tragedy (p. 61)**
*Matching*
1. b   2. e   3. a   4. c   5. d
*Fill in the Blanks*
1. 300
2. Sierra Nevada

3. Sutter's Fort
4. 47
5. youngest

**Brigham Young (p. 64)**
*Matching*
1. d   2. c   3. a   4. e   5. b
*Fill in the Blanks*
1. Vermont
2. Mormonism
3. Twelve Apostles
4. Joseph Smith
5. Great Salt
*Constructed Response*
grow extra crops; store food; build wagons; made arrangements for temporary quarters in Missouri for other converts from the United States and England who would later join them in Utah

**The End of the Trail (p. 65)**
Preemption Act of 1841: allowed each male settler to claim 640 acres of land; additional 160 acres could be claimed for a wife and each child
Homestead Act of 1862: head of family or single person over 21 allowed to claim 160 acres of public land by paying a $34 fee, if they lived on it and cultivated it for five years

**Traveling by Stagecoach (p. 68)**
*Matching*
1. e   2. a   3. c   4. d   5. b
*Fill in the Blanks*
1. weapons, blankets, water
2. window
3. nine
4. overturn
5. month

**The Pony Express (p. 70)**
*Matching*
1. b   2. d   3. e   4. a   5. c
*Fill in the Blanks*
1. ship, stagecoach
2. 100
3. 1860
4. stations, riders
5. 5

**Morse Code (p. 72)**
1. The telegraph was a great invention.

**Homes of the Settlers (p. 75)**
*Matching*
1. d    2. b    3. a    4. e    5. c
*Fill in the Blanks*
1. earth
2. heat, droughts
3. 160
4. sawmill
5. together

**Major John Wesley Powell (p. 77)**
*Matching*
1. b    2. c    3. d    4. e    5. a
*Fill in the Blanks*
1. New York
2. Union
3. ropes
4. two, 538
5. Mormon

**Word Search: What Did They Take? (p. 78)**

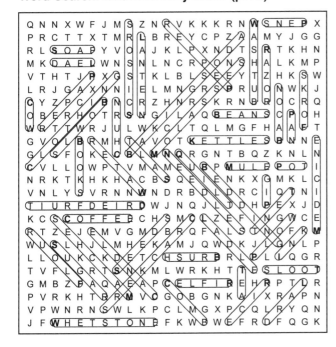

**Unit Three: Gold Rush**

**Gold Rush Time Line Activity (p. 83)**
A. 6       B. 8       C. 2       D. 5       E. 1
F. 7       G. 10      H. 9       I. 3       J. 4

**What Is Gold? (p. 85)**
*Research*
1. 79
2. Au
3. Transition Metals

4. solid
5. metal
6. natural
7. stable

**Gold Discovered at Sutter's Mill (p. 86)**
*Cause and Effect*
Possible answers include:
1. The California Gold Rush began.
2. The area had enough citizens to become a state in 1850.
3. Merchants could get rich quicker than miners.
4. Vigilantes took the law into their own hands.

**John Sutter (p. 88)**
*Matching*
1. b    2. a
*Multiple Choice*
1. b    2. c

**The Forty-Niners (p. 91)**
*Research*
1. The Golden Fleece
2. They traveled a long way in search of gold.

**Tools of the Miner (p. 97)**
*Matching*
1. c    2. e    3. b    4. d    5. a
*Fill in the Blanks*
1. Ames
2. cheated
3. essentials
4. belt
5. Candles, oil

**Rocking the Cradle (p. 99)**
*True or False*
1. T    2. T    3. F    4. F    5. T

**Using a Long Tom (p. 100)**
*True or False*
1. F    2. T    3. T    4. F    5. T

**Staking a Claim (p. 103)**
*Matching*
1. b    2. c    3. a    4. d
*Constructed Response*
Codes helped miners who found gold in an area. When a miner found traces of gold, he could stake a claim to the area. This gave him the exclusive right to search for gold there. If there were no codes, anyone could look for gold on someone else's claim.

**Women Strike It Rich (p. 105)**
*True or False*
1. T    2. F    3. F    4. F    5. T

**Gold Rush Justice (p. 108)**
*Matching*
1. b    2. a    3. e    4. c    5. d

**Black Bart (p. 110)**
*Matching*
1. c    2. e    3. d    4. b    5. a

**San Francisco (p. 112)**
*Fill in the Blanks*
1. San Francisco
2. gold
3. scavenged
4. saloons
5. West

*True or False*
1. T    2. F    3. T    4. F    5. F

*Cause and Effect*
Possible answers include:
1. San Francisco became the fastest growing city in the world.
2. Many merchants made more money than miners.
3. The town was created in a haphazard fashion with poorly constructed buildings.

**Search for the Gold (p. 115)**

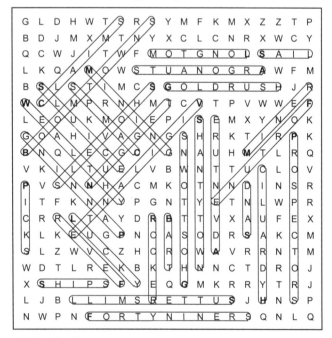

1. football
2. San Francisco